THE EYE OF SHIVA

THE EYE OF SHIVA

SHIVA

*Eastern Mysticism
and Science*

Amaury de Riencourt

WILLIAM MORROW AND COMPANY, INC.
New York   1981

Library of Congress Cataloging in Publication Data

Riencourt, Amaury de.
    The eye of Shiva.

    "Morrow quill paperbacks."

    Bibliography: p.
    Includes index.
    1. Mysticism.   2. Religion and science—1946-
I. Title.
BL625.R5   1981   291.1'75   80-22032
ISBN 0-688-00036-3
ISBN 0-688-00038-X (pbk.)

Printed in the United States of America

2   3   4   5   6   7   8   9   10

For my Father

ACKNOWLEDGEMENTS

I am gratefully indebted to the following authors and publishers for permission to reprint material from their works:

Pantheon Books, a division of Random House, Inc., for permission to quote from *The Way of Zen* by Alan W. Watts; and from *Zen in the Art of Archery* by Eugen Herrigel.

Cambridge University Press, for permission to quote from *Science and Civilization in China,* vol. 2, by Joseph Needham; and from *Physics and Philosophy* by James Jeans.

Oxford University Press, for permission to quote from *Science and the Common Understanding* by J. Robert Oppenheimer.

George Allen and Unwin Ltd., for permission to quote from *The Autobiography of Bertrand Russell* by Bertrand Russell.

Harper & Row, Publishers, Inc., for permission to quote from *Physics and Beyond* by Werner Heisenberg, World Perspective Series, ed. Ruth Anshen, © 1971 Harper & Row, Publishers, Inc.; and from *Physics and Philosophy* by Werner Heisenberg, World Perspective Series, ed. Ruth Anshen, © 1958 Werner Heisenberg.

Pandit Gopi Krishna, for permission to quote from his book, *Kundalini.*

CONTENTS

"The only channel through which we can have a glimpse of this hidden creation, of this invisible world of consciousness and intelligence, is ... the all-seeing Eye of Shiva which can penetrate to the hidden levels of existence impervious to normal sight."

Gopi Krishna
Yoga, a Vision of its Future

THE EYE OF SHIVA

INTRODUCTION

At 5.30 on the morning of July 16, 1945, in a desert area known as the Jornada del Muerto in the Alamogordo air base, a stupendous white flash tore apart the sky, dazzling and blinding a small group of scientists ten thousand yards away. The enormously bright ball of fire grew steadily larger as if to wipe out the atmosphere and engulf the world, leading some terrified scientists into believing that they had lost control of man's first nuclear explosion. At this very moment, an apparently incongruous incident took place: Robert Oppenheimer, director of the Los Alamos Scientific Laboratory and prime coordinator of the atomic experiment, began to hum some stanzas he had read years before when he was studying Sanskrit:

> *divi sūrya-sahasrasya bhaved yugapad utthitā*
> *yadi bhāḥ sadṛśī sā syād bhāsas tasya mah'ātmanaḥ*

> If the radiance of a thousand suns
> Were to burst into the sky
> That would perhaps be like
> The splendour of the Mighty One.

An imaginative description of a possible nuclear explosion? Far from it; in fact, it was a poetic rendering of the explosive nature of mystical ecstasy written thousands of years ago on the banks of the Ganges: the Mighty One, emanation of the Godhead, grants an awe-struck Arjuna his first staggering insight into the mysteries of the inner Self.

As the gigantic nuclear cloud mushroomed up to the stratosphere followed by a doomsday roar, Oppenheimer continued with the verses in which the Mighty One reveals Himself:

> I am become death
> The shatterer of worlds.

Then and there, Oppenheimer symbolized a most extraordinary conjunction—the juxtaposition of Western civilization's most terrifying scientific achievement with the most dazzling description of the mystical experience given us by the *Bhagavad Gītā*, India's greatest literary monument.

Ironically, this scientific accomplishment destroyed one of the basic premises that had started Western scientific thinking on its course some twenty-five centuries ago in Greece: the integrity and indivisibility of the atom. In splitting it and releasing its inner energy, Western science did more than devise man's most awesome weapon; it also symbolized the destruction of the psychological assumptions on which the Greek philosopher Democritus and, much later, Isaac Newton based their view of the universe—the existence of a material, indestructible and eternal *atomos* as fundamental building block of the material universe.

No one who was alive and conscious in 1945 when nuclear power was at last harnessed could doubt that mankind had reached a historical watershed in terms of technological power. But what few saw was that it was a watershed in more ways than one—that it was also a great divide in man's long religious evolution. Oppenheimer's spontaneous conjunction of a Hindu mystical poem with a nuclear explosion was of great symbolic significance. Nowhere in Western literature could he have found an almost clinical description of mystical rapture that *also* fits the description of a nuclear explosion in the outer world. Could this be mere coincidence, or does it point to some profound convergence of man's inner subjective and outer objective worlds? And does it also point to some hidden convergence of the development of Eastern mystical insight and Western scientific knowledge, concealed behind the apparent divergences?

We are obviously faced here with a triangular problem which is going to be the theme of this work: confronting both Eastern and Western cultures with the philosophic implications of contemporary physics. Clearing away all the deadwood that stands in the way—outdated myths and outworn ideas—we will reach some tentative conclusions as to the fate of religion in the planetary civilization of the future.

1 SCIENCE AND RELIGION

Our point of departure lies quite naturally in the fact that it is easier today for the thoughtful man to have a spiritual outlook on life than it was a century ago. In an apparent paradox, it is the scientific revolution of our century that makes it possible. There was a time, not so far back, when it seemed that an iron-bound deterministic science was about to establish a complete dominion over man and his environment, when the universe was seen as a cosmic machine functioning according to mathematical equations; the physical world was seen through the lenses of an engineer and the mind was thought to coincide with the brain. All this is now water under the bridge and the contemporary physicist regards the material world "in a more mystical though no less exact and practical way," in Arthur Eddington's words.[1]

Strangely enough, there is also, in what some call this post-Christian world, a profound and rising scepticism regarding the dogmas and theologies of Western creeds—although man's religious aspirations are greater now than they were two or three generations ago. God is by no means dead, as a recent tradition from Nietzsche to contemporary theologians would have us believe; but the Christian God is shifting from the distant stratospheric "Heaven" and the Biblical past into man's subjective being. The God of the West is now "in the gut," where it has always been in the Eastern tradition. The belief in a "beyond" in time and space is being metamorphosed into a belief in the deep, timeless here and now. That type of Western man who is a harbinger of spiritual trends no longer projects outwardly but is beginning to look for some ultimate reality within himself, within his unconscious and its deeper layers which often appear to him to plunge right through the material universe.

The evidence points to the fact that we are indeed crossing a historical watershed, comparable in scope to the birth of Christianity some two thousand years ago. A new spiritual vision is beginning to take shape under the spur of a most paradoxical alliance between the new physics of the twentieth century and Eastern, rather than Western, mystical insight. Few physicists who reach the outer limits of their science can avoid taking a side-glance at the *meta*-physical implications of the recent scientific revolution; but the surprising fact is that contemporary science, in its search for a philosophic framework, seems to be deliberately turning away from its cultural roots, finding a more compatible atmosphere in the totally alien metaphysics of the Orient. It is the startling similarity between the world-picture of today's physics and the world-vision of Eastern metaphysics that is perhaps the most outstanding cultural phenomenon of our times.

In other words, a new planetary culture is coming into being; the obvious Westernization of the East is part of the process; and so is the Orientalization of the West, although it is taking place in a more subtle way. This Orientalization involves a steady retreat from all the dogmas and theologies inherited from the Western past, a discarding of all the trappings of formal and conventional religion, a growing disbelief in myths, symbols and metaphors masquerading as historical "facts." This religious withdrawal from the objectified "outer" world which is now wholly abandoned to science implies a deepening of man's concern with his own inner self where he is likely to find the mainspring of happiness and suffering, hope and despair, belief and doubt. But, in the new vision of the universe shaped by contemporary physics, is there any room for an autonom•ous self, for God, spirit or soul?

The same steady retreat from conventional religion and institutionalized Churches beaten by the Western spiritual metamorphosis, was beaten early in the twentieth century by the science of physics when it began to withdraw from the familiar world of sense-perceptions into an increasingly abstract mathematical description of the universe. As a result, this new picture of the physical world is absolutely baffling. Contrary to classical science, physics now states without ambiguity that the commonsensical world in which we live simply does not exist; all our impressions of ulti-mate solid substances are deceptive. The scientific revolu-tion of the past decades has shattered all our previous notions of physical reality and natural law: space, time, energy, matter and causality have all acquired different meanings. And yet, in the second half of the nineteenth century, it seemed that physics had reached its ultimate stage: the two great elements of the material world, light and matter, appeared to be thoroughly known and under-stood: matter was made of atoms, light of waves. This was universally accepted by scientists with dogmatic assurance.

However, late in the last century, the first cracks in Newton's mechanical model of the universe began to show along with premonitory rumblings of the scientific earth-quake to come. The notion of matter as something sub-stantial whose building blocks, the atoms, were presumed to be the ultimate indivisible constituents of the material world had earlier suffered a body blow when Michael Fara-day discovered that the atom contained particles of elec-tricity. Ernest Rutherford had followed this up by finding out that the atom was made up of a nucleus and electrons whirling around it as if it were a miniature solar system with its revolving planets.

But the true beginning of the revolution took place in the study of radiation where, in order to solve some intractable problems, Max Planck put forth his audacious Quantum Theory in 1900. According to it, there existed a fundamental and irrevocable discontinuity, where it was least expected, in the exchange of energy between an elementary material system (atom or molecule) and the radiation of light and heat—in other words, there were no intermediate energies between two neighbouring energy levels. Planck's theory therefore ascribed an atomicity to radiation similar to that of matter and described the discharge of radiation from matter as being discontinuous, metaphorically not as "in a steady stream like water from a hose, but rather like lead from a machine-gun."[2] These bits and pieces of radiation were dubbed *quanta* by Max Planck. This amazing discontinuity went a long way to explain the remarkable stability of matter under the impact of external influences, ". . . a pure miracle when considered from the standpoint of classical physics," claimed Niels Bohr who eventually connected Rutherford's model of the atom with Planck's quantum of energy.

Meantime, another revolutionary development was taking place, from quite another angle. Young Albert Einstein published in 1905 a paper establishing the foundations of the Special Theory of Relativity. Rejecting the then prevailing theory of space as a fixed framework in which an infinite number of individual particles were externally related to one another, moving along a totally unrelated time dimension, Einstein postulated that the universe was one single, unbroken four-dimensional continuum—three dimensions of space and one of time—lacking the Newtonian flow of time: different observers will see events occurring in different temporal sequences according to their respective positions and velocities: there was no more universal "now." His colleague, Hermann Minkowski stated at the time that "From henceforth space in itself and time in itself sink to mere shadows, and only a kind of union of the two preserves an independent existence." [3] Niels Bohr pointed out subsequently that in classical physics the statement that two events were simultaneous was considered a wholly objective fact. Today, we have to accept the new fact that "simultaneity" includes a subjective element since two events may appear simultaneous to an observer at rest but not necessarily to one in motion. [4] And so, out went the rigid separation between the objective and the subjective that had been a marked feature of Western thought since the ancient Greeks began to philosophize.

Einstein further established a new universal law: the velocity of light is the highest, and limiting, velocity in the physical universe. And whereas classical physics had assumed that the mass of any physical object was fixed and unchangeable, his Theory of General Relativity (1915) postulated that it increases along with the increase in velocity, reaching theoretical infinity if the object attained the speed of light. Not only that; gravitation ceased to be considered an external "force"; it became part of the physical body's inherent inertia whose course is determined by the metric properties of the space–time continuum in which it moves. In addition, the old classical notion of a rigid distinction between energy (active and without mass) and matter (concrete, inert and endowed with mass) disappeared: Einstein proved conclusively that matter is simply condensed energy—therefore that matter and energy are interchangeable. More startling still, gravitation was found to be endowed with the ability to *bend* light, implying that the universal space–time continuum is actually curved and bends back on itself to describe a gigantic cosmic sphere.

This complete overthrowing of the notion that space conforms to Euclidean geometry leads to a new and bewildering picture of a boundless, yet finite universe which physicist James Jeans compares to the four-dimensional *surface* of a corrugated soap-bubble consisting of three dimensions of space and one of time—adding that the *inside* of this cosmic sphere, that is the substance out of which the bubble is blown, the soap-film, is a combination of empty space and empty time—a void.[5]

In this new Alice-in-Wonderland universe, Relativity implies that space–time itself *is* the metrical field and cannot exist without structure or curvature; in turn, the greater or lesser degree of curvature depends at that particular point upon the presence of a greater or lesser amount of matter. This enfolding of the space–time continuum upon itself generates elementary particles which are basically temporary creases or wrinkles in the fabric of space–time. The increasing interweaving of such wrinkles produces, by further enfolding, the far more complex structure of an atom ... and so on, rising ever higher in the degrees of complexification.

The new universe disclosed by Einstein's Relativity presents itself as a continuous whole made up of interrelated *events*, prompting Alfred North Whitehead to state that "The event is the unit of things real."[6] These events are determined by the geometric properties of the "field" where they occur. Classical physics had conceived of an empty space extending indefinitely in all directions and an equally empty time without beginning or end, but totally separate from space; both were presumed to be pre-existent to matter, both logically and, by implication, chronologically. No more. This universe of classical physics has been swept away by Relativity whose main hallmark is *unification*, joining together in an indissoluble continuum space, time, energy and matter.

One of the latest theoretical discoveries or hypotheses in astrophysics appears to put some kind of a capstone on the present scientific vision of the physical universe, as the logical and inevitable result of Einstein's Theory of General Relativity: the notorious "Black Holes" in interstellar space which seem to tear apart the fabric of space–time as a result of the gravitational collapse of dying stars and into which everything material disappears without a trace, elementary particles as well as giant stars, and from which light itself cannot escape (making them utterly invisible), pointing out in bold relief the ephemerality of "matter" itself. In such a "singularity," as scientists call it, one of which appears to exist in the constellation Cygnus and another in Scorpius, time and space simply evaporate beyond its "event horizon," compressed out of existence by the infinite density and gravitational force of the catastrophic collapse. It appears that multitudes of them puncture the four-dimensional spheric universe as they would a round lump of Gruyère cheese with its holes; some scientists assert that there are more than a million of them in our galaxy alone. No direct information can be got out of them since light itself cannot escape. But then, what is on the other side of these "event horizons" which, in effect, would mark one of the terminal boundaries of the physical universe? In strictly material terms, nothing. That would presumably be the interior of James Jeans' "soap bubble" consisting of "empty space welded onto empty time."

We are, indeed, very far from Newton's model of the universe. In just a few decades, scientific thought has moved many light-years away from the classical physics of the nineteenth century.

Somehow, Relativity had to be connected with the Quantum Theory, its major partner in the scientific revolution. And so, Einstein began to conjecture that *all* forms of radiant energy travel in discontinuous quanta and postulated that light itself is composed of particles which he named *photons*; that left the proponents of the old venerable theory that light was made up of waves quite puzzled because many experiments with light involving diffraction and interference can *only* be explained by the wave theory. Ultimately, which was it, particles or waves? The question has never been answered, except by stating that it is both. And this was only the beginning; it was soon discovered that this fundamental dualism affects all of physical nature. In 1925, Louis de Broglie put forth the theory that the interactions between matter and radiation could only be explained by postulating that electrons were *not* individual particles but systems of waves or wave-packets. So it was that the scientific revolution, having extended the corpuscular concept to radiation without repudiating its wave-like character in certain instances, was now, in a reverse process, dematerializing matter by ascribing to its elementary constituents wave-like features!

It soon became clear that all elementary particles could be interpreted as waves as well as granular elements—it made no difference to the mathematical equations that dealt with them since they are not substantial *things* in the commonsensical meaning of the term. James Jeans points out that a substantial material sphere occupies a definite position in space and a certain amount of room—while an electron does not. Ever the master of apt metaphors, he adds that it is as meaningless to attempt to find out how much room an elementary particle occupies as it would be to locate a fear or an anxiety in space–time![7]

The new wave mechanics developed by Erwin Schrödinger gave mathematical shape to this inherent dualism and triggered Niels Bohr's Theory of Complementarity according to which any physical event can be interpreted in two different frames of reference, mutually exclusive, yet also complementary in the sense that *both* are needed to give the true picture: it is only through their juxtaposition that the phenomenon can be really understood. At the microcosmic level, the objective, familiar world of space and time ceases to exist; the mathematical interpretation of this subatomic world no longer refers to actual reality, but only to potentialities. Max Born eventually appropriated Schrödinger's mathematical expression for the wave function and baptized it a statistical "probability"—the probability that the intensity of a given part of the wave was a rough indication of the possible distribution of particles in that area. So that, in the final analysis, material waves became merely "probability waves." And to add to the complexity of the new physics, while the waves of a single electron can be represented in three-dimensional space, the waves of two electrons require a six-dimensional space, and a nine-dimensional space is needed for three electrons, and so on *ad infinitum*.[8]

At this point, the ultimate material reality that physics can apprehend is the "field" and in the aspect of the quantum field, it is both a continuum and a discontinuum, the discontinuities being temporary condensations of space–time where the field is unusually intense, giving rise to corpuscular matter. Einstein put it bluntly in stating that in the new physics, there is no longer room for both the field and matter because the field is the only reality.[9] In fact, particles are merely fields in interaction and their mass and other supposedly inherent properties simply emerge from their interactions with other particles—the "being" and the "happening" now coincide.[10] Events and movements of waves or particles presuppose that "something" is in motion ... but what is it? It was eventually hypothesized that this "something" was a *psi field*, with which concept the evaporation of the notion of concrete matter became complete. A noted physicist points out that while it was believed, in the nineteenth century, that all interactions involved material things, this is no longer considered to be true. It is now accepted that there are completely nonmaterial fields, described by some of the most important equations of quantum mechanics—fields that can be as abstract as the square root of a probability.[11]

With Werner Heisenberg's Principle of Indeterminacy (or Uncertainty), we now reach the outer limits of scientific possibilities by doing away altogether with determinism and rigid causality in view of the impossibility of determin-

ing simultaneously the position and velocity of a particle—
the greater the precision of the one, the greater the im-
precision of the other. The deeper we penetrate into the
microcosmic world, the more difficult, if not impossible,
the direct observation. We may see in a cloud-chamber the
condensation trail left behind by an electron that has
broken loose from an atom; but the electron that remains
inside the atom will always remain unobserved and unobservable.[12] Arthur Eddington explains that while the
readings truly reflect the fluctuations of the world qualities,
our real knowledge is that of the readings rather than of the
qualities—and the readings resemble the qualities as much
and as little as a telephone number resembles a subscriber![13]

In addition, the observation itself *interferes* with the behaviour of the phenomenon. For instance, let us suppose
that an imaginary microscope was able to magnify an individual electron a hundred thousand million times so as to
make it visible to the human eye; since an electron is smaller
than a light wave, the scientist could only make it visible by
using radiation of shorter wave-length. This would imply
using high-frequency gamma rays of radium that would push
the electron around so violently as to make an objective study
of it impossible. So it is that the Principle of Indeterminacy
reinforced Niels Bohr's Theory of Complementarity in finally
destroying the classical physics' faith in the possibility of
exact calculations, leaving us with "probability" calculations as our only mathematical tools at the subatomic level.

This amounts to saying that physics can go only so far
and no further in its objective study of nature because it
collides with an ultimate barrier set up by nature itself—
taking into account the limitations imposed by our sensorial apparatus. Beyond, there remains a whole realm of
"reality" that can *never* be investigated by scientific observation. Physics has to presuppose the existence of a
background or substratum that shall forever remain outside the scope of its probings because, as Heisenberg him-

self pointed out, ". . . we cannot make observations without disturbing the phenomena—the quantum effects we introduce with our observation automatically introduce a degree of uncertainty into the phenomenon to be observed."[14] And when the margin of uncertainty is calculated, it turns out that it is always a function of that greatest of all mysteries: Max Planck's constant quantum, h.

Physics is now reduced to statistical statements and pointer readings (index needles, scale readings, photometers, oscilloscopes, sensitive plates, speedometers, cloud chamber observations). Physical laws now simply express the "connectivity" of these pointer readings.[15] All they give us is *indirect* evidence. What we can observe are only the *traces* of collisions or interactions—they are, themselves, unobservable; and what happens *between* interactions is even more unobservable. And, to go one step further, we cannot even assume that unobserved events follow the same laws as observed ones because quantum mechanics has clearly established that they do not—they do not follow the postulates of causality. Not only do we have to accept the substitution of "probability" for exactitude and certainty; we also have, here, to deal with outright *causal anomaly*, that is a clear violation of causality, a much more grievous blow than mere probability, which definitely breaks down the applicability of causality in the microcosmic world.[16] The law of radioactive disintegration proposed by Rutherford and Soddy in 1903 asserts that atoms of radioactive substances break up spontaneously without preliminary conditions or happenings—so that we have now effects without causes![17]

Ultimately, what this scientific revolution leaves us with is the fact that the Theory of Relativity shows that we can observe only *relations*, while the Quantum Theory has determined that we can observe only *probabilities*. Both together result in the following: all the mathematical equations that handle particles or wave-packets in their different states or conditions do not actually represent them at all;

they merely indicate the different kinds and amounts of *knowledge* we may have about them.[18] Thus, modern physics has become essentially epistemological, and has given up all claims (if it ever entertained any) to be ontological; it deals with the grounds of possible knowledge, not with the essence of a fundamental reality that is beyond its scope. The net result, as James Jeans points out, is that ". . . the ultimate processes of nature neither occur in, nor admit of representation in space and time,"[19] and he elaborates:

> . . . the fundamental laws of nature do not control the phenomena directly. We must picture them as operating in a substratum of which we can form no mental picture . . . Events in this substratum are accompanied by events in the world of phenomena which we represent in space and time, but the substratum and the phenomenal world together do not form a complete world in itself which we can observe objectively without disturbing it. The complete closed world consists of three parts—substratum, phenomenal world and observer.[20]

To sum up, the world we see and experience in everyday life is simply a convenient mirage attuned to our very limited senses, an illusion conjured by our perceptions and our mind. All that is around us (including our own bodies) which appears so substantial, is ultimately nothing but ephemeral networks of particle-waves whirling around at lightning speed, colliding, rebounding, disintegrating in almost total emptiness—so-called matter is mostly emptiness, proportionately as void as intergalactic space, void of anything except occasional dots and spots and scattered electric charges.[21] For instance, any single one of the roughly 10^{27} atoms of the average human body is already minute enough—in decimal notation its average diameter of one or two Ångströms is about 0·0000000001 metre. Yet, although almost all of its mass is concentrated in the nucleus, the radius of this nucleus itself is one hundred thousand times smaller[22]—so small, in fact, that if all the nuclei of all the atoms that make up the whole of mankind were packed tight together, their global aggregate would be the size of a large grain of rice![23] An atom, therefore, is almost completely empty space in which minute particles whirl around within its confines at speeds of up to forty thousand miles per second—enough to make us dizzy when we grasp the fact that, in the last resort, that is what our physical bodies and everything material are ultimately made of. And, as we shall see later,* even this is only an approximation to the truth inasmuch as, in quantum physics, an object may be split into its constituent parts but does *not* consist of them!

A Victorian scientist thought that he knew clearly what he was talking about when he mentioned atoms, matter or energy; he visualized them as tangible and describable components of the great universal cosmic machine. But this mechanistic interpretation was nothing more than a philosophical background, a psychological predisposition which did not find any actual support in strict physical facts and theories. Lord Kelvin, for instance, asserted that he could understand nothing if he could not make a mechanical model of it—hence, not surprisingly, he never did understand the revolutionary electromagnetic theory of Maxwell.[24] In those days, the predominant mechanist-materialist outlook had assumed an uncritical metaphysics whose concepts unjustifiably hypostatized a strictly material universe outside of which there was presumed to be no reality, just as dogmatic religion, in previous, centuries, had "spiritualized" and "miraculized" it.

Today's physicist knows that this Victorian outlook is no longer tenable. In fact, science no longer pretends to have anything to say about the intrinsic nature of the universe. Scientific knowledge is all inferential knowledge. Physics presents us with a symbolic skeleton of the universe at-

*See p. 170.

tuned to our senses, couched in mathematical formulas, not with an accurate picture or objective description of the universe itself. James Jeans has claimed that "The universe begins to look more like a great thought than a great machine."[25] And he added:

> The concepts which now prove to be fundamental to our understanding of nature—a space which is finite; a space which is empty, so that one point differs from another solely in the properties of the space itself; a space which forever expands; a sequence of events which follows the laws of probability instead of the laws of causation—or, alternatively, a sequence of events which can only be fully and consistently described by going outside space and time, all these concepts seem to my mind to be structures of pure thought, incapable of realization in any sense which would properly be described as material.[26]

The one undisputable fact about the universe we know is human *consciousness* which is known to us by direct and immediate self-knowledge. Physics now accepts the fact that we have to restore consciousness to the fundamental position in the universe, rather than see it simply as a secondary material epiphenomenon derived from a particular arrangement of atoms and particles in the brain. Arthur Eddington asserts that:

> Recognising that the physical world is entirely abstract and without "actuality" apart from its linkage to consciousness, we restore consciousness to the fundamental position instead of representing it as an inessential complication occasionally found in the midst of inorganic nature at a late stage of evolutionary history.[27]

Physicists such as Eugene Wigner, for example, believe that the formal inclusion of consciousness in physics could well become an essential feature of any further advance in our scientific understanding.[28] Our mind is the one element of knowledge that is not limited to pointer readings; obviously, only consciousness can provide the necessary background for all the pointer readings which, in the aggregate, constitute physical science.

This background is mind-stuff and as Eddington puts it, the "stuff of the world is mind-stuff." [29] This mind-stuff is not spread out in time and space; on the contrary, it is time and space that are spun out of it. Here and there it rises to the level of self-consciousness in human beings and from those tips of icebergs floating on the periphery of the world-stuff springs our two-tier intellectual knowledge— direct knowledge within each thinking individual and generalized inferential knowledge which includes that of the physical world. [30] Inferential knowledge, however, is only part of a whole and cannot grasp the whole; science cannot, regardless of further progress, encroach on the background or substratum from which it springs; and our consciousness obviously lies in this background—indeed, *is* the background.

We are thrown back, by physical science itself, onto the problem of the nature of consciousness—or rather, our task now is to deal with that part of consciousness that does not emerge in space and time, and is therefore not amenable, and never will be, to scientific analysis. [31] Could it, perhaps, be handled by the insights of the religious or spiritual approach?

Sometime in 1927, probably the most crucial year in the development of the new physics, Wolfgang Pauli, one of the most eminent scientists and a pioneer in quantum physics, told Werner Heisenberg what he thought of the so-called conflict between science and religion:

> ... it was precisely the idea of an objective world running its course in time and space according to strict causal laws that produced a sharp clash between science and the

spiritual formulations of the various religions. If science goes beyond this strict view—and it has done just that with relativity theory and is likely to go even further with quantum theory—then the relationship between science and the contents religions try to express must change once again. Perhaps science, by revealing the existence of new relationships during the past thirty years, may have lent our thought much greater depth.[32]

It has, in a true sense. On the one hand, by taking over completely the material world as perceived by the senses, science has at last confined religion strictly to the non-material realm. But by admitting its inherent inability to penetrate the "background" out of which matter springs and into which it eventually dissolves again, it has given up all claims to compete with religious belief in whatever lies in this background. According to Arthur Eddington, "... religion first became possible for a reasonable scientific man about the year 1927 ... If our expectation should prove well founded that 1927 has seen the final overthrow of strict causality by Heisenberg, Bohr, Born and others, the year will certainly rank as one of the greatest epochs in the development of scientific philosophy."[33]

This is a new departure in man's history inasmuch as throughout its course, what we term religion has always been inextricably mixed up with magic, witchcraft, art, morality and rudimentary science. In the Middle Ages, for instance, men gave miraculous or teleological explanations for every natural phenomenon—earthquakes, storms, eclipses. They sought God's purpose rather than natural causes in phenomena. Scientific knowledge and ignorance being what they were, the Church felt compelled to pass judgement on matters that had no bearing on the core of religious belief—the controversy between geocentric and heliocentric theories of astronomy, for instance; and was put on the spot when proved wrong by an awakening physical science. Each defeat of this kind contributed to increasing disbelief in the dogmas of formal religion. It was not just a matter of particular denomination or Church. In religious matters, Martin Luther was a revolutionary; but a few years after Copernicus published his scientifically revolutionary *De Revolutionibus Orbium Coelestium* in 1543, Luther blasted him for wanting to prove that "the Earth is moved and goeth around and not the sun," adding that this was "the over-witty notion of a Fool, who would fain turn topsy-turvy the whole Art of Astronomy."[34]

It was this intrusion of clerical authority into non-spiritual affairs that eventually produced the great clashes between science and religion in the following centuries. But the plain fact is that at no time did scientific progress ever *disprove* the hard core of religious belief in the West, that is what is left of spiritual faith when stripped of all its unnecessary adjuncts. And yet, the psychological fact is that the rise of modern science did lead to a profound wave of religious scepticism in the past two or three centuries. The collapse of the Church's dogmatic positions in mundane matters which were irrelevant to the life of the spirit splashed over religion as a whole. Newton's scientific outlook made the universe look like a cosmic machine in no need of a God Almighty, let alone a personalized one. Even Newton, a true Christian believer, worried about the fact that it appeared as if God the Creator no longer had anything to do in the gigantic universal machinery that operated like clockwork. What was left of the idea of an extremely remote and indifferent Lord made Him seem totally irrelevant to the lives and sorrows of men. Whether God existed or not made no real difference. Newton tried to cling to the idea that the Almighty did, from time to time, interfere in natural processes and occasionally corrected the irregularities of misbehaving planets and stars; he insisted, for instance, that ". . . the diurnal rotations of the planets could not be derived from gravity, but required a divine arm to impress it on them."[35] But when Laplace showed conclusively that they were all self-correcting, a further blow struck religion as a whole: science would no longer accept the slightest supernatural cause in the physical universe. And when reproached by Napoleon for failing to mention God in his monumental work on celestial mechanics, Laplace replied, "Sire, I have no need for that hypothesis."[36]

The decline of belief in an effective God had a marked impact on another component of Christian faith: the teleological nature of the world. Belief in a world-purpose was part and parcel of Western culture; that too went out the window when Newton's purposeless world-machine took over. Throughout the following two centuries, the mechanical interpretation of physical nature swept the Western world. Hobbes, Hume and countless other philosophers propagated this world-view which made a teleological explanation quite as unnecessary as faith in an effective God: the universe was stripped of its spiritual meaning and purpose.

The fact that this trend of thought was quite illogical is irrelevant. Physical science is bound, by its very nature, to be mechanistic since it interprets phenomena by means of causality and natural laws—even when, at the limit, it has to give them up. Even the new physics of our century do not explain anything by way of purpose and volition. Inevitably, in the collective mind of Western public opinion, teleology became unscientific and in the popular imagination anything unscientific was deemed unreal. The idea of a Divine purpose in the world faded away. And just as religion had, in previous centuries, invaded non-spiritual areas that were none of its concern, science now took over its pre-eminence and, in a reverse process, began to invade areas of belief that could never belong to it—as we now know in the light of contemporary physics. There is no point in quoting chapter and verse of all that was written and proclaimed in the name of a certain "scientism." The following remarks of Sigmund Freud sum them all up:

> The scientific spirit engenders a particular attitude to the problems of this world; before the problems of religion it halts for a while, then wavers, and finally here steps over the threshold. In this process there is no stopping. The more the fruits of knowledge become accessible to men, the more widespread is the decline of religious belief, at first only of the obsolete and objectionable expression of the same, then of its fundamental assumptions also.[37]

Wolfgang Pauli is correct in hinting that it took the scientific revolution in the midst of which he was working and to which he contributed so much, to restate the respective spheres of science and religion—which old Victorian Freud could never begin to understand. But, by and large, the philosophical implications of this revolution have not yet percolated down to the world of Western philosophy, art and literature where meaninglessness and despairing purposelessness still hold full sway. And so, the progeny of religious illusion became the father of agnostic disillusion.

Finally, the last major component of Western creeds had to collapse along with the teleological concept: the idea that the world is a moral order, that the Divine power ruling the world is a righteous one, striving to instil moral goodness in man. From being objective, moral values have shifted to being largely subjective and the world-process has become totally detached from morality. Ethical values are intimately connected with purpose; obviously, if the universe is purposeless, no moral value or design can attach to it. As Dostoyevsky noted, if God does not exist, then everything becomes permissible. Furthermore, if the universe is a cosmic machine entirely under the sway of rigid causation, is there any room left for free-will? And, if not, how can there be any objective morality?

The existence, throughout a shrinking world, of a great many different religions, often contradicting one another, has added its contribution to the confusion and decline of spiritual belief. The great advantage of science is that it is *one*. It speaks the same language all over the world, uses the same signs and symbols; an equation will mean the same thing to any scientist regardless of nationality or cultural background. This is not the case with institutionalized religions, each one of which has its own symbolism and metaphorical language, often exceedingly obscure to the non-initiate. Therefore, the problem is to attempt to penetrate to the hard core of *all* religions, and stripping them ruthlessly of their mythological wrappings, discover whether they contain a kernel of truth which they all hold in common—which could then be called the religious view of the world—and which could, under no circumstances, collide with the scientific picture of the universe.

A great many creeds and Churches scattered throughout the world claim a near-monopoly of spiritual truth with a remarkable lack of the metaphysical humility that characterizes contemporary physics. It has obviously become difficult for any thoughtful person to subscribe to any such exclusive claims, whatever they may be. All religions are at once true and false, in the sense that they all seem to point to some ultimate truth, but that none of them is literally and absolutely true. All their myths, dogmas, Scriptures and theologies are merely symbolic and relative interpretations designed to help the devotee on his spiritual way.

A spiritual *way*—this is the one thing all religions have in common, a way of life. The ways may be and are different; but the first outstanding characteristic of religion in general is the fact that it is more than a set of beliefs about God, the soul, heaven and hell: the religious life implies a total commitment of the devotee over and above his intellectual creed. A Christian is not only one who believes in the divinity of Christ; it is one who lives, as best he can, the total life of a Christian—mere intellectual commitment to a theological doctrine is not enough. This helps explain why a set of beliefs can appear incongruous to the layman who does not *live* them, while appearing perfectly natural to those who do actually live them and whose unconscious is in tune with their symbolic meaning. In any dedicated religious life there is a compound of intellectual commitment, transrational belief, volition, emotion and sentiment, which varies from one religion to another, but is always present.

Spearheading the way are the great saints and mystics who often appear to lead superhuman or transhuman lives and who seem to know the "way" because they have travelled it and reached some sacred destination—be it the Christian who heeds Jesus' admonition according to St. John's Gospel: "I am the way ...", or the Buddhist who follows the "Noble Eightfold Path," or the Taoist and Confucianist who see (in different ways) in the Tao the path that every Chinese must follow in life, or even the Hindu who reads in the epic *Mahābhārata*: "Hard is the great path (*mahāpanthā*) and few are they who travel it to the end."[38] This "way" is the way of the mystic, and its destination is mysterious, ineffable, that is literally beyond verbal description, inexpressible in any language, although it can be hinted at in pictures and metaphors, music and poetry. As Dante expressed it in *La Divina Commedia* when describing his own Beatific Vision, "Now shall my speech fall farther short even of what I can remember than an infant's who still bathes his tongue at breast."[39] This way and its destination—heaven, salvation of the soul, freedom from rebirth, Nirvāna, return to Brahman or whatever—however differently expressed, is what all religions have in common. And it is here, in the direct records of the personal experiences of the great mystics, that the heart of the religious impulse is to be found, rather than in the official dogmas and conflicting intellectual interpretations of philosophers and theologians.

This is the hard core of *all* religions because, fundamentally, there is only one way and one ultimate destination, only one fundamental experience, however differently conceived and expressed in various religions. Gifted mystics attempt to describe this experience for the benefit of the less endowed laymen who try to follow them on the sacred path. Basically, the mystical experience is one and often breaks through the thin cultural coating which tradition and education have bestowed on the mystic; those who have experienced this unfathomable "oceanic feeling" of depth beyond depth, this otherwordly rapture, are often irresistibly tempted to abandon the world altogether and plunge forever into this mysterious supernal "beyond," leaving the rest of mankind to its blind fate.

Perhaps one of the most dramatic instances of the contrast between intellectualized faith and actual mystical experience is given us by Thomas Aquinas whose monumental *Summa Theologiae* remained the philosophic cornerstone of Roman Catholic theology for centuries. On the day of the Feast of St. Nicholas in 1273, he was unexpectedly overpowered by an ecstasy of such intensity that he began to weep and sob; in one instant, all his remarkable theological writings appeared to him to be totally worthless. In his own words, he had now come to realize that "Everything that I have written seems to me like straw, in comparison with the things that I have seen and that have been revealed to me."[40] And, thereafter, never wrote another word. This, from a theological standpoint, rather embarrassing episode, illustrates the staggering nature of mystical rapture, not only as physical sensation and spiritual emotion, but also as translogical *knowledge* of a far higher order than can be acquired by the most brilliant analytical intellect—presumably direct knowledge of that mysterious background of pure consciousness, undetermined and undeterminable, that ultimate reality of which physics can tell us nothing, save that it exists. This noetic quality is certainly one of the main characteristics of mystical insight whose transrational knowledge is always imbued with an overpowering sense of transcendental authority. It is striking that the great nineteenth-century Hindu mystic Śrī Rāmakrishna expressed himself in almost the same terms as Aquinas: "One cannot get true feeling about God from the study of books ... books, Scriptures and science appear as mere dirt and straw after the realization of God."[41]

Quite clearly, all religions have sprung from this undefinable potential in human nature that appears to transcend its physical limitations, a potential awareness made actual in some peculiarly gifted human beings. And it is in the sumtotal of the records of their own direct personal experiences in this realm beyond life and death, and beyond time and space that the kernel of religious truth is to be sought and found—although in most men, this mystical disposition lies far beneath the threshold of waking-consciousness, not strong enough to break into the open and revolutionize their lives.

It has by now become clear that there can be no real conflict between science and religion, if by science one implies contemporary physics and by religion, mysticism. In fact, they appear to complement one another in an unexpected application of Niels Bohr's theory of Complementarity. Few prominent physicists are mystically inclined, but many are concerned about the religious problem as a whole and they would probably concur with Einstein when he stated the following:

The most beautiful and most profound emotion we can experience is the sensation of the mystical. It is the sower of all true art and science. He to whom this emotion is a stranger, who can no longer wonder and stand rapt in awe, is as good as dead. To know that what is impenetrable to us really exists, manifesting itself as the highest wisdom and the most radiant beauty which our dull faculties can comprehend only in their most primitive forms—this knowledge, this feeling is at the centre of true religiousness.[42]

Coming from the most eminent scientist of our century, this moving expression of spiritual emotion should give food for thought to all those sceptics who suffer from tunnel vision.

What concerns us now, however, is the outstanding cultural phenomenon of our times—contemporary physics finding a more congenial *meta*physical extension in the mystical vision of the Orient than in the blurred vision of Occidental metaphysics. Anyone concerned with this phenomenon should read Erwin Schrödinger's essay on Vedānta, the paramount philosophic expression of Indian metaphysics. Schrödinger is remarkably well equipped from a scientific viewpoint to formulate this synthesis and he finds plenty of "support for the basic Vedantic vision, chiefly by pointing out particular lines of modern thought which converge upon it," in his own words.[43] What does this East–West cultural rapprochement imply for the future of religion?

Quite obviously, if this potential convergence becomes actual, some consequences will also become evident. In the first place, it must be kept in mind that the twentieth-century revolution in physics is more than just another scientific revolution: it is also a prodigious expansion of the scientific understanding of the universe which stretches from the infinitesimally small to the infinitely large; it does not actually abolish the Newtonian structure but overcomes and preserves it as being only a *special case* within the much larger framework provided by Relativity and Quantum Theory. The Newtonian concepts still apply within the realm of everyday life where their rough approximations are valid, but break down as we move away from the familiar world of ordinary sense-perceptions into an increasingly abstract and penetrating mathematical description of the fundamental constituents of the universe—that is, as we come closer to the very edge of the material world. The significant point, as we shall see later, is that the intuitive vision of the East saw and sees this ultimate physical reality in contemporary twentieth-century scientific terms rather than in Newtonian ones.

In the second place, it then becomes obvious that there would be an objective validity to the general mystical experience when stripped of all the mythological trappings of the various cultures and religions in which it is expressed. This would amount to a mutual confirmation of the latest scientific revolution and the overall mystical experience. It might also indicate areas of potential collaboration between scientists and mystics if a connection between their respective frames of reference can be established.

Our approach will take into account the basic components of both the Eastern and Western types of consciousness which underlie their respective groups of Higher Cultures, starting from the original matrix out of which they both sprang: the magic mind.

2 THE MAGIC MIND

As far back as one goes in Palaeolithic times, man was immersed in a mental universe of magic, a dreamlike world in which man's unconscious prevailed absolutely—a world without calendar, coming historically from nowhere, going nowhere. The remarkable fact is that this magic *weltanschauung* is by no means dead today; it can still be found in scattered pockets of primitive life throughout the world—among some Australian aborigines, for instance, whose concept of *aljira*, "dream-time" or "ghostland," also the "time when there was no time" characterizes this archaic world-outlook based on a projection of the contents of the unconscious.[1] It also lives on in the unconscious of us all, immersed in that vast psychological ocean out of which spring all the symbols of our night to night dreamworld, as the primitive reptilian part of our brain, seat of instinctive impulses, subsists alongside the far more evolved cerebral cortex. And in some odd way, the magic mind already gives us a faint whiff of the spirit of both Eastern metaphysics and modern physics.

What concerns us is the inner structure of that magic world-picture as it displayed itself openly in those remote days, unchallenged by what we know today as rational and scientific thought—a world in which the law of cause and effect did not apply, a world of perpetual transmutations in which forces operating between things are *inherent* in them rather than external. Magico-primitive thinking has no notion of an objective world separated from the observer; it bases its world-picture on man's inner experiences, on the

THE MAGIC MIND 43

world of the psyche, including all its emotional and volitional components. In other words, in this world-outlook,
everything, animate and inanimate alike teems with life—
life is everywhere in everything. There is no basic distinction between man and nature, no opposition—man is thoroughly embedded in mother nature;[2] all he understands is
life as a universal stream of existence in which he is only an
unindividualized drop, without autonomous personality.
For instance, the Chinook Indians in northwest America
will render the following sentence, "The evil man has killed
the poor child," into "The wickedness of the man has
killed the poorness of the child."[3]

All natural phenomena are understood in terms of human
experience, and human experience is viewed as a natural
phenomenon. This implies that magic man lives in a seemingly chaotic world of endless metamorphosis, where phenomena lack identity with themselves and are rarely what
they appear to be, where the image of a thing becomes
identical with the thing itself. This projection into the outer
world of man's ability to undergo inner transformation and,
sometimes with the help of narcotics and drugs, the wearing of masks, dancing, music and witchcraft, to alter his
levels of consciousness, leads straight to this universe of
ceaseless transmutations which climaxed, much later, in the
pursuit of alchemy. What was important was the actual
psychological experience, not the facts as such. For instance, ". . . the mask in a primitive festival is revered and
experienced as a veritable apparition of the mythical being
it represents—even though everyone knows that a man
made the mask and that a man is wearing it. The one wearing it . . . does not merely represent the god; he *is* the
god."[4]

This magic world-picture was the result of the injection
of the shifting symbolism of dreams and psychoses into
what we, today, perceive quite clearly as the external objective world. Living in close communion and harmony with

an unconscious that was not repressed by rational thought, magic man saw the world replete with things and phenomena that had not condensed into permanent and definite shapes; the same applied to his own dreamlike mind. There was no sharp distinction between animate and inanimate, physical and psychological. Man might become beast or god, animals could be metamorphosed into deity or man, and deity could take on human or animal shape. Phenomena were not ruled by implacable *laws* but were the symbolic expression of human or extra-human *will* and capricious interference.[5]

In other words, magic man did not face the phenomenal world as an *it* as we do, but as a world of multiple personalized *thous*[6]—a world replete with wilful living entities, so overwhelmed with life that death was not conceived as the natural negation of life but as a transition from one form of existence to another, usually brought about by the will of some supernatural agent or witch-doctor. There was no precise distinction between the living and the dead; survival of the dead was implicitly assumed since their memories affected the living and lived on in their minds. Death was more than a transition to another form of life, actually—it was a concrete reality in its own right that was opposed to life which should normally be eternal. Death was a phenomenon confronting another phenomenon, endless life.

In fact, this world of *thous*, capricious and accidental, was generated by psychological forces reacting to the ill-understood impact of natural phenomena. Thou is personalized, unrelatable to any law, unpredictable as life itself and knowable only insofar as it chooses to reveal itself. Knowledge is not emotionally detached but *participatory*, intuitive in the sense of sharing in the being of *thou* in a reciprocal relationship that is always dynamic. Nothing is inanimate, the world overflows with life—everything, storms, earthquakes, floods, all natural happenings were individualized and personified with their own specific will and character; they were not looked upon with intellectual detachment but were experienced in the sense of human life facing non-human life, infra- or super-human, as the case may be. As a noted anthropologist put it, "For the primitive man, everything is a miracle, or rather, nothing is; and therefore everything is credible, and there is nothing either impossible or absurd." [7]

The magic universe, just as man's unconscious, is one of symbolism in which symbol and thing symbolized were both involved in a dynamic relationship, in which the symbol did not merely represent but actually shared in the being of the thing symbolized. Symbolism was essentially *effective*, a form of action rather than just a form of knowledge—as when names of enemies were erased or their reproductions destroyed, the intention being, not merely to express a feeling or a wish, but to actually perform a magic operation that must result in concrete injury. Only those—sorcerers, witch-doctors, shamans or high-priests—who could read the symbolic structures of the universe could understand these complex connections and perform accordingly. The world was understood in terms of networks of fields of forces in which the objective and subjective poles were almost non-existent, a world of dynamic relationships between symbols and things symbolized, in which the things, in turn, were seen as symbols themselves on another level—in which senders and receivers changed place every so often but remained forever in a continuous life-stream made up of interconnecting lines of life-forces.

Man did not think merely with his mind; the whole man, imaginative, intuitive, emotional, volitional *experienced* these dynamic relationships; all happenings were individual affairs which could not be explained rationally but were interpreted by means of legends and myths rather than logical analysis. Men actually experienced conflicts of supra- or infra-human powers on the outcome of which their very existence depended, and they embodied in these myths the wisdom culled from these experiences, myths which were not mere allegorical entertainment but possessed the unquestioned authority that scientific laws have for us today. Myth was not an abstract statement to be disputed by a rational mind but a compelling truth beyond dispute because it was actually *lived*. More than that, the telling of the myth and its dramatization by means of play-acting, poetry and music was not merely the conveying of a truth but the actual means whereby it was *brought about* concretely by involving these extra-human powers in the specific developments of the world.

The apex of the magic world-outlook was reached with astrology, this pseudo-science which truly raised the magic mind above the merely primitive and made it into the most comprehensive mental structure in those distant times. Originating among the Chaldeans, this complex structure of criss-crossing influences (originally signifying the cosmic power pouring down to earth from sidereal bodies) was viewed as determining or at least influencing the course of terrestrial events and the fate of men. Being dynamic power-houses in their own right, astral bodies each had their own specific powers and influences. But planets and stars were not the "causes" of the fate of those they influenced; they were simply involved in a relationship based on sympathetic magic which constituted an indissoluble phenomenon linking celestial body and man.

In short, "being" in the magic conception consisted in influencing and being influenced in a complex world where symbols represented interweaving influences. Everything was connected with everything else in this criss-crossing pattern; nothing was a matter of indifference. Most important in this *qualitative* view of things, man was conceived as a "microcosm," a world of its own, fully comparable with, and also symbolic duplication of the entire universe itself— the great "macrocosm"—and not just a part of it. The natural correspondence of microcosm and macrocosm entails the principle that "the part stands for the whole," *pars pro toto*—whether it be part of the body, the shadow, even the name of a person.[8]

Everything being based on correspondences and affinities in a universal life-stream teeming with significance, there was no room for detached and unemotional speculative thinking. Symbolic thought in the magic universe was entirely *practical*, not theoretical. Thought could not be emotionally detached and disinterested; it was intensely involved because all forces operating between things were inherent in those things and there could be no sharp separation between observer and phenomenon observed. A causal relationship, on the other hand, is emotionally indifferent and *external* to those things that are linked by it; but the causal thought-process was impossible in the magic framework which ignored completely the existence of a separate objective world, a mental framework in which all knowledge is based on inner psychological experience; and that experience was the only thing that mattered, the only reality that counted since dreamlike existence had as much, if not more, reality as external phenomena perceived during the waking state.

In this magic framework, in fact, reality was not one. There were *degrees* of reality, the degrees rising with the strength and intensity of the *subjective* impact. The hierarchical structure of the cosmos was based on the rising degrees of reality, itself closely connected with the greater or lesser influence and permanence of the phenomenon's impact, and consequently with the greater or lesser value of the interconnection. The dynamic nature of a world-picture made up of endless transmutations implied an upward or downward movement along the scale of reality; the greater or lesser reality of a thing depended upon the intensity with which it affected feeling, thought or will—which is why dreams could be, often, far more important than waking-state perceptions, and therefore that much more real. In the magic outlook, efficiency was the keynote: to be, is to be effective.

Magic knowledge ignored the sharp separation between subject and object, both merging into one another as a result of sympathetic understanding. The purpose of thought and knowledge was to lead to action on things and beings through sympathetic magic—itself based on the two fundamental principles of *similarity* (like attracts like), whereby magic man can produce what he wants by imitating it, and *contagion* according to which contiguity principle his manipulation of an object will influence whoever was or will be, at some point, in physical contact with it.[9] Magic man never analyses his mental processes nor does he care about the abstract principles or laws underlying his knowledge; magic thought is never autonomous and its logic is essentially implicit, not explicit.

Magic knowledge is basically self-knowledge, a deliberate, wilful and emotional participation in the phenomenon and a partial identification with it. Knowledge is worthwhile only to the extent that it is simultaneously influence, that it *acts*. Sympathy and empathy, surrender of the personality in order to live the life of an alien being or entity, allows magic man to reach an intuitive awareness of the essence of things and therefore to influence them from the inside, so to speak. In fact, it is really the knowing observer who undergoes transformation rather than the object of knowledge.

Scientific knowledge proceeds the other way, isolates the phenomenon under investigation in order to act upon it without in any way altering the observer himself. Magic man cannot, and would not, move far away from perceptual reality does not look for impersonal laws, asks "who" rather than "what," sees deliberate and capricious will involved in every phenomenon and looks for its symbolic meaning. This also implies that celebrations and rituals are not mere symbolic performances but are actual *part of* all the cosmic events that are being celebrated; thus does man act out his preordained part in cosmic life, emphasizing the necessary coordination between himself and the play of natural forces.

In short, magic thinking is the obverse to conceptual thought's reverse. Neither time nor space, for instance, are abstracted as general categories and homogeneous entities.[10] Magic thought views space as a heterogeneous medley of concrete orientations, time as an equally heterogeneous collection of recurring phases of greater or lesser duration—days and nights, seasons, childhood, adolescence, maturity and old age, each with its own specific significance and value. Times and spaces have their emotional connotations—east is birth and life at sunrise, west is death at sunset. Everything is viewed under the qualitative and concrete aspect rather than the quantitative and abstract. Even the changes of seasons and the movements of stars and planets were looked upon essentially as life-processes correlated with those of men; and not merely natural processes but processes generated by one or several wills, eventually personified and attributed to various deities.

Beyond the interaction of wills, however, the movements of the world were also viewed as forming a vast network of dynamic correlations and fields of forces in which, as pointed out earlier, the objective and subjective pole were completely overshadowed by the all-important correlations: living in a world where the unconscious projected itself freely and where conscious thought was still at a minimum, magic man saw inanimate as well as animate entities behaving like himself, like men, partaking of their own lives. In short, all those qualities which, later, became the exclusive prerogative of man were viewed as belonging to all things under the sun—hence magic man's profound feeling of affinity for his environment. Belief in ceaseless transmutations deprived magic man of any sense of permanent identity, a man whose contours were blurred and faded imperceptibly into his environment.

The existence of a form of rudimentary mysticism in the magic world is a fact, corroborated by archaeological and anthropological evidence. This proto-mystical impulse is often present among sorcerers, medicine-men and shamans of present-day primitives, crude, unrefined, but obviously the remote ancestor of the far more profound and enlightened mysticisms of the Higher Cultures. Magic mysticism is not only rooted in the primitive magic mind, it probably *originated* its whole mental outlook and is sharply distinguished from the evolved mysticism of the Higher Cultures by the following features: in the first place, it is mostly orgiastic rather than ascetic and relies predominantly on natural or artificial excitement of the nervous system; it includes all sorts of taboos and often relies on self-inflicted suffering which triggers an exhalted state of rage. This contrasts with the bliss induced by various forms of intoxication with the assistance of drugs, often followed by singing and dancing which lead to a state of self-hypnosis.[11]

These various techniques usually generate in their devotees states of cataleptic ecstasy which seem to be devoid of any element of intellectual ravishment which characterizes evolved mysticism. Far from inducing self-integration and synthesis, they produce a disintegration of whatever personality there is in the primitive; the "I" splits into so many heterogeneous components and this eventually leads to outright insanity. All this often characterizes the first steps of the civilized mystic, although he strives to overcome this morbid phase—whereas magic man tends to remain there. We can see this initial phase of dissociation in St. Theresa of Avila or St. Paul, but they soon leave it behind. Magic mysticism aims toward a morbid state, toward neurosis rather than sanctity.

What is clearly lacking in magic mysticism is a strong feeling of love, along with a definite lack of intellect and morality. The sexual element predominates in it whereas it is sublimated in civilized mysticism. Furthermore, magic mysticism lacks any kind of intellectual discrimination and abandons itself freely to all the disintegrating influences induced by its orgiastic nature. This, evidently, is due to the magic atmosphere itself which prevents primitive man from being master of himself, since he can conceive of no self to master, no power of wilful concentration, no individual life, no coordination of ideas and no self-identity. He is incapable of introspective analysis and is wholly given to irrational impulses. On the whole, it is a spineless form of mysticism, totally invertebrate, completely dependent on emotions and physiological reactions.

The difference between magic and higher mysticism finally boils down to this, that "magic wants to get, mysticism wants to give," which is all due to the lack of feeling of love in the magic world. Whereas in magic the will unites with a primitive and rudimentary intellect in search of knowledge and power over countless forces, deities or demons, in mysticism the will unites also with loving emotion in order to transcend the sensuous universe.[12]

Sometime toward the end of the Neolithic, a profound psychological revolution began to take place, at first sporadically, and then at an increasingly fast pace: man's ego became self-conscious and gradually separated itself from its environment, shattering the magic world-picture; its outlook made up of criss-crossing correspondences and interrelations between entities of the same nature was destroyed by the rising self-awareness of the conscious ego, a revolutionary change in man's mental outlook. The first task of the rising ego is to *integrate* the human personality, hitherto split into various shifting components always subject to endless transmutations. This integration, eventually, allows the ego to separate itself mentally from its environment and assert its autonomy and self-identity as well as its unity. The newly assertive "I" swallows and absorbs the semi-independent components of its personality, cuts them off from their natural extensions in the external world and brings the entire personality under its control.

In turn, this condensation and crystallization of the ego ruptures the complex network of dynamic forces and becomes, for the first time, an autonomous, integrated centre in its own right. Transmutations and metamorphosis come to an end, things and beings assume clearer, more distinct and permanent shapes; dynamic forces previously endowed with life become neutral, lifeless forces: man no longer faces a living, wilful *thou* close to him, but a lifeless, inorganic *it* completely external to him, indifferent and remote.

In the magic universe, living and thinking are one, the latter being merely an instrument of survival, designed practically to enhance life. Now, having shattered the magic world-picture in which all the emphasis was put on dynamic *relations* which absorbed the objective and subjective poles in one phenomenal unit, man reorients himself in such a way that the poles begin to emerge in full clarity and autonomy, and move away from one another. Out of the ruins of this magic world-view, the internalized subject and the external object both arise from their former obscurity in the ruling unconscious to become the main entities in the glaring light of the now ruling conscious mind. Simultaneously, thought itself becomes increasingly autonomous and begins to sever its connections with the rest of the human being, including its feelings and emotions, striving for the cold detachment of *abstract* thinking.

Integrated and assertive, the ego then proceeds to deal with the *it*. In the magic universe where all things were presumed to be of the same substance and teeming with life, divinity was *immanent* in nature, underpinning life and the phenomenal universe. This religious outlook lasted in the Middle East, for instance, until the beginning of the second millennium B.C. It was slowly and gradually destroyed when Hebrew monotheism introduced the absolutely *transcendent* Godhead which puts Him beyond and above nature and physical phenomena. There is now no divinity whatsoever in nature, no immanentism or pantheism of any kind—nature becomes completely profane. God is pure Being, immensely remote, the fount of all values which drastically devalue both man and nature. God transcends all phenomena, yet is the ground of all existence. In fact, the Hebrew Almighty is the first example of total abstraction—although not completely out of the clutches of the *I–thou* relationship yet, since Yahweh became the one and only *thou* facing man. True enough, the universe, natural phenomena, plants, animals, everything had now become an *it*, but all the *thous* that were expelled from man's natural environment now condensed into one supreme, gigantic, absolute *thou* whose name was Yahweh. Hebrew culture, in fact, did not really come to grips with the *it*. This achievement was the work of the Greeks.

3 EAST AND WEST

Out of the disintegrating remains of the magic world-out-look arose the two great forms of consciousness that are still with us today, each of them generating a cluster of Higher Cultures and religions, East and West, Orient and Occident. The East incorporates all that derives, basically, from Indian culture: Hinduism, Buddhism and their extensions in the Far East and Southeast Asia. The complementary unity-in-diversity of that vast area springs from the fact that while Indian philosophy and wisdom is the most profound, its most perfect means of expression are to be found in the artistic achievements of China, Japan and Southeast Asia (Angkor, Borobudur). The West includes all that derives from Greek thought and Hebraic experience—in other words, Judaism, Christianity and Islam. While there was, historically, a great deal of overlapping and mutual interpenetration along the fringes of the two great groups, they remained, by and large, side by side as remarkably distinct entities, impermeable to one another as if they were located on different planets, even when geographically contiguous.

The increasingly self-conscious and emancipated ego now dominates the field of human consciousness in all civilized lands, from Spain to China, and proceeds to set up two entirely divergent mental structures on the ruins of the magic outlook. A choice between two possibilities is open to it: it can either confront the *object* as an opponent in order to overpower and master it, and therefore *objectivize* both the external world and itself: the path of extroversion, the Western solution as devised originally by Greece's Ionian philosophers. Or, again, the ego can focus on the inner being that underlies it, in a process of introversion, and seek out the pure *subject*, the deep Self, virtually dismissing the object as ultimately unreal—the Eastern solution. As the Mahāyāna Buddhists put it metaphorically, "Just as a pearl-hunter, aided by heavy stones tied to his feet, dives to the bottom of the ocean and secures the precious pearl, so should man, aided by indomitable will, dive deep within himself and secure the most precious of all jewels," the Self (*antar-ātman*).[1] In this Eastern context, the sage discards the objective world and, turning his mental gaze inward (*pratyag*, "into the interior"), reaches the underlying subject, which he identifies exclusively with the real.

The Western form of consciousness invests the object with all the trappings of reality. The object itself (*objectum*, "that which is thrown against the subject") stands unalterably opposed to the subject as that which has to be mastered and overpowered by the Promethean ego; the objectifying process tends to absorb everything since it can see no limitations of any kind; it encompasses not only the external world of physical phenomena and human perceptions but also the internal world of mental activity, ideas and concepts. Mental abstractions, religious entities, theologies, philosophies and scientific theories are all objectified, that is conceived as existing *independently* of the thinking man—with the result that Western man has, over the past twenty-five hundred years, filled his mind and the visible universe with an increasingly complex array of objects held together by rational thought. Even the Almighty was objectified and set up above an equally objectified soul. Ultimately, as Erwin Schrödinger reminds us, scientific "comprehensibility is bought at the price of letting the subject recede, which makes objectivation possible."[2]

The Eastern form of consciousness, retaining from the

magic picture that which it felt valid, refused to sever completely the object from the subject, while shifting its centre of gravity to the sovereign subject. In this context, the object (*viṣaya*) was not allowed to evolve into an autonomous entity that could threaten the integrity of the subject (*viṣayin*)[3]—in other words, was not allowed to evolve into an object at all and was granted only a temporary degree of reality: what stands for the object in Eastern consciousness is simply the alien non-subject—the "not-Self" (*etat*) of the *Upaniṣads*[4]—which is ultimately destined to dissolve into a fog of total unreality, once the subject has come to know itself. This alien non-subject is the world of *nāma-rūpa*—*nāman* being the world of names, ideas and concepts corresponding to the physical world of perceived "forms," *rūpa*. *Nāma-rūpa* implies therefore the whole phenomenal world, made up all at once of the thinking individual with his mind and sense-perceptions as well as all the external objects and phenomena. All Eastern schools of thought, from Vedāntic Hinduism to Mahāyāna Buddhism agree that the ultimate goal of knowledge lies well beyond the phenomenal world of *nāma-rūpa*.

In this Eastern context, the real is the subject—not the superficial ego (*ahaṅkāra*), which is part of the alien non-subject that must eventually be eliminated, but the deep Self (*ātman*) which lies far beyond the threshold of the conscious mind and which is reached when stripped of all its non-subjective elements like barnacles from a ship's hull. The bond between subject and alien is much closer in the East than the antagonistic connection between subject and object in the West—this closeness being such that all forms of autonomous existence of the not-Self must be viewed fundamentally as unreal (*māyā*), which encompasses both physical phenomena and mental activity. Inevitably, the dismantling of this illusion becomes the main goal of the Easterner's striving for ultimate Self-realization. In the *Chāndogya Upaniṣad*, the teacher Prajapati "tries to bring out the absolute supremacy of the subject over the object, the truth of Yajñavalkya's statement that even when all objects are extinguished, the subject persists in its own light: 'When the sun has set, when the moon has set, and when the fire is put out, the Self alone is his light.' " [5]

The Chinese, less mystically inclined, were more tempted to emphasize the essential *polarity* between Self and not-Self, which they call "other." In a commentary of Hsiang Hsiu and Kuo Hsiang on the *Chuang Tzu* (The Book of Master Chuang), they state that:

> There are no two things under Heaven which do not have the mutual relationship of the "Self" and the "other." Both the Self and the other equally desire to act for themselves, thus opposing each other as strongly as east and west. On the other hand, the Self and the other at the same time have the mutual relationship of lips and teeth. The lips and the teeth never (deliberately) act for one another, yet "when the lips are gone, the teeth feel cold." Therefore the action of the other on its own behalf at the same time helps the Self. Thus though mutually opposed, they are incapable of mutual negation.[6]

Objective thinking made its first decisive appearance in Greek pre-Socratic philosophy, and the process of objectification can be best understood by looking at the rare surviving fragments of Heraclitus of Ephesus. Up to his time, as a legacy of the magic mind, dream-pictures were considered to be more real than mental activity in the waking-state—in other words, the unconscious was granted a higher degree of reality. This hierarchy was turned upside down by Heraclitus:

> It is therefore necessary to follow the common. But while reason is common, the majority live as though they had a private insight of their own ... Those who speak with a sound mind must hold fast to what is common to all ...

The waking have *one* common world, but the sleeping turn aside each into a world of his own.[7]

Clearly, the implication here is that man's rationality must hold on to what is *common* to all in the waking-state, to what Heraclitus calls *koinón* or *xunón*, which was, on the other hand, contemptuously dismissed in the East, under the Sanskrit name *vaiśvānara*, as being far *less real* than the dream-state in which the subject is cut off from the rest of the world. This Eastern attitude conforms to Carl Jung's estimate that "I have to admit the fact that the unconscious mind is capable at times of assuming an intelligence and purposiveness which are superior to actual conscious insight."[8] Everyone of us can experience this fact for himself.

Thus it is that the Greeks initiated the Western withdrawal from the appreciation of the unconscious, focusing more and more on the objectified external world seen by waking-consciousness: only *that* is real, whereas the subjective world of dream-consciousness became an illusion—anything disparagingly dismissed as "subjective" implying fundamental unreality. This amounts to excluding the cognizing subject from the objectified picture of the world and setting the basis of a scientific world-view: this evaporation of the knowing subject, this exclusion of the subjective and the unconscious from the realm of reality became the hallmark of the Western outlook. As a result, neither sense-perceptions such as sounds, colours or tastes, nor the consciousness that registers them directly appear in the objectified picture of the physical world; they are replaced by correlated abstractions such as chemical reactions or electromagnetic vibrations—and yet, all such abstractions are ultimately based on those very sense-perceptions that are kept out of the objective picture. Man, as ultimate subject, disappears from the framework of cognition and yet he is the ultimate fact—you, I, all thinking and feeling human beings that are really the sole concern of the East. It is left to Erwin Schrödinger to provide the link between the two world-pictures:

> Actually, one can say in a few words why our perceiving self is nowhere to be found *within* the world-picture: because it itself *is* the world-picture. It is identical with the whole and, therefore, cannot be contained in it as a part.[9]

This is, and has always been, the standpoint of the East, a conclusion to which a contemporary physicist is bound to come on the very frontier of the objectified universe. This objectified universe is the product solely of waking-consciousness, of Heraclitus' domain "common to all."

Walking in Heraclitus' footsteps, Parmenides, another Greek philosopher, was the first one to state unambiguously that "thinking" and "being" are identical: "Thought is the reality in which the whole of being is actualized as such." He and his followers presumed that in rational thought they had the actual presence of the whole of being and absolute truth: "They concluded that this gave them the right to repress by violence any other thinking that might lay claim to truth."[10] Hence was born the dogmatic intellectualism, the ideological slavery to the abstract *idea*, that has haunted Western thought and behaviour to this day. It was not until Kant that Western philosophy was able to begin to get out of this mental straitjacket and separate abstract thought from being. At any rate, both Heraclitus and Parmenides stand on the threshold of Western philosophic thought, and stamped it with their objectifying spirit. As Karl Jaspers remarks, "Their work is permeated by exclusion, antagonism, a furious aggressiveness. There is a despotic spirit in both men."[11]

So it is that Greek man looked out of himself, rather than within, looked out at the external world, nature and the universe, attempting to understand its objective structure, but ultimately failed in the attempt. As Democritus expressed it, "Colour is by convention, sweet by convention, bitter by convention; in truth there are but atoms and the void." But he also saw the danger of intellectual arrogance gaining the upper hand and imagines sense-perceptions replying to the rational intellect: "Wretched mind, from us you are taking the evidence by which you would overthrow us? Your victory is your own fall."[12]

Thrown back upon himself, Greek man began to look at man's relationship with the universe, at the meaning of life and destiny within an objectifying framework; but the speculative physics of Ionian philosophers, from Thales to Anaximenes—objectifying nature-philosophers, all of them—could not reach the decisive intellectual certainty they all craved. Then came Socrates who did not pursue their line of inquiry but raised new questions they had never thought of—the validity of knowledge and its "purpose"; in the objectifying context set by his predecessors, however, these questions could not be answered. The problem was that in such a context, man had been reduced to being merely an object among other objects; they had dehumanized the universe and had lost sight of the specificity of the subjective human being; and in spite of the Delphic Oracle's command, *gnothi seautón*, "know thyself," (Sanskrit *ātmānam viddhi*, "know the Self"), actual knowledge of the Self had become impossible because of the elimination of the subjective as being ultimately unreal: only the objective was knowable and there was no longer a Self to be known. It never occurred to Greek idealism's naïveté that the human mind's limitations could restrict it to mere appearances—it assumed uncritically that the rational mind could cognize the whole of reality and that this reality was the external world of physical phenomena, along with the discursive thinking that comprehends it.

The relative failure of the pre-Socratic attempt sprang from its growing realization that sense-perception data alone produces unreliable information—as Democritus has already informed us. The investigating mind eventually had to face itself and reach the conclusion that the only valid source of knowledge was mental cogitation in the form of rational and logical thought. From then on, the source of all the problems that have plagued Western philosophical thought should have become apparent: from Parmenides, who equated being with pure reason and logical thought, through Descartes' famous *cogito, ergo sum*—"I think, therefore I am"—to Hegel's affirmation that the real is the rational and the rational the real (*vernunft = wirklichkeit*), the Westerners took the view that consciousness coincides largely with *rational* thinking, the product of waking-consciousness only. Progressing from the disappointing and unreliable *percept* given us by our sense-organs to the abstract *concept*, Greek thinkers elaborated one theory of the objective universe after another, until they reached the grandiose conception of Plato's theory of Ideas—ideas alone are objectively real and pre-exist their discovery by man; though purely mental, they are the ultimate objects, of which the visible and tangible objects of the world are only imperfect replicas. Objective Idealism thus identified reality with the pure object, that is with the result of rational thought of which the physical world of phenomena is only a pale shadow. This basically secular and proto-scientific approach to the investigation of objective reality did away completely with myth and mythology, radically severed the object from the subject by isolating the former for investigative purposes; rationality was to be the sole guide in this effort to grasp the objectively real. From then on, conceptual thought began to lead an autonomous life of its own, divorced as much as possible from sensations, instincts, emotions and especially from the repressed and ill-understood unconscious. This was not only the work of the philosophers; even tragedians like Euripedes came to the conclusion that truth is to be found only in literal objective fact rather than in symbol, and rejected mythology as historically inaccurate, hence *objectively* untrue; he ended up destroying Greek tragedy which had been, until then, the sole outlet for the dramatic symbolizing of Greek mythology.

In the Eastern view, searching for some kind of reality, either in the physical world (*prakṛti*) or in the rational mind (*manas*) is a sheer waste of time since they are both ultimately unreal. The fundamental problem of Eastern consciousness is to bring about the *identification* of the Self with the Ultimate Subject—that is, the identification of *ātman* with Brahman, the Godhead. Tantric meditational techniques, for example, direct the seeker to visualize, at first, a divine image and then to "identify" with it; this is based on the premise that "one cannot venerate a god unless one is a god oneself" (*nadevo devam arcayet*), implying the actual awakening and recovery of one's own inner divinity.[13] Whereas the fundamental problem of Western consciousness is one of *relation* between sharply distinct entities, the objectified human soul and an equally objectified God Almighty perceived as an external *Deus ex machina* or, better still, as the *totaliter aliter*, the "Wholly Other," the Supreme Object.

In historical terms, the basic divergence between East and West became manifest in Mesopotamia in the second millennium B.C. when the divine and human realms, hitherto fused together, split away from one another. The king or ruler lost his inherent divinity and became the humble servant-priest of a transcendent, and no longer immanent, deity. The problem now became one of relationship between man and an external god, rather than identification with it, in the Eastern fashion. This objectifying trend, religiously anticipating the forthcoming Greek philosophizing one, started in Babylonia under Semitic auspices. The increasing transcendence of the Almighty, the growing distance separating gods and men culminated in the Bible, as we have already seen. But nowhere in pre-Biblical Babylonian religious literature is there any reference to the mystical impulse, to the existence of a Divine essence *within* man; the Divine is wholly and completely transcendent, never immanent. The gods dwell in the sky or underground, never in the hearts of men—in Sumero-Babylonian cuneiform script, the sign for deity was a star.[14]

In the East, the process was reversed—man *is* potentially divine and all he has to do is to strip away the veils of ignorance (*avidyā*) created by the phenomenal material world and the mental activity that goes with it; he must dispel the unreal world of *māyā* in order to reach identification with his true, timeless Self. In the East, ultimately, there is no objectified Godhead, no supreme Lord that exists in and for itself, no cosmic Creator of the universe, no permanent external divinity nor imperishable soul that is more than a convenient and wholly temporary symbolic prop: the Godhead is your own, deep, concealed, unindividualized and transpersonal Self. And not beyond death, in some distant heaven or other, but right here and now; as the *Brihadāranyaka Upaniṣad* states it, "*Today* also, he who knows this—I am Brahman—becomes the universe; and even the gods have no power to prevent his so becoming; for he *is* its *ātman*."[15]

In the West, the sharp separation between the human and Divine spheres triggered a longing for the re-establishment of the broken connection between the two. The end result of this spiritual longing was the birth of the concept of *linear* history as a spiritually meaningful and purposeful progression in time with a beginning and an end, process in which the Will of God reveals itself. The cosmic process now appears as a directional unfolding with a once-and-for-all Creation *ex-nihilo*, followed by a Fall (Original Sin), a struggle to overcome it and reach Redemption. The West looked for what theologian Paul Tillich calls the "New Being" *in* the historical process itself rather than *beyond* it; it looked upon history as a development of unique and unrepeatable events, all endowed with ethical meaning. History acquires a spiritual and metaphysical significance as being the main battleground on which the dramatic and ceaseless struggle between the forces of good and evil takes place. As Martin Buber put it, "In Babylon the cult calendar might carry on its eternal cycle above and immune to the vicissitudes of history; in Israel history with its own hands transcribed the calendar into the stupendous signs of the unique." [16]

All this is utterly foreign to the basic concepts of the East where the ever-recurring *cycles*, either historical in China or transhistorical in India with its endless revolving *yugas* and *mahāyugas*, prevailed. The process of historical development, in this context, has no spiritual or metaphysical significance whatsoever. In fact, one of the main concepts of the East, the transmigration of the soul, or rather of the subtle body (*sūkṣma*), automatically deprives history of any kind of spiritual meaning by replacing its collective drama with a purely *personal* series of developments through the births and deaths of the individual. There is no temporal tension here, no historical struggle between good and evil, but a natural and inevitable *alternance* between two complementary poles, as between night and day. In China, for instance,

> Instead of observing successions of phenomena, the Chinese registered alternations of aspects. If two aspects seemed to them to be connected, it was not by means of a cause and effect relationship, but rather "paired" like the obverse and the reverse of something, or ... like echo and sound or shadow and light. [17]

This is, of course, perfectly symbolized in China by the pairing of the two fundamental and complementary emblems, *yin* and *yang*. In India, we also find this complementary pairing, but in a more religious context, in the two apparently contradictory aspects of *śakti*, the primordial cosmic energy which displays itself either as the goddess Durgā, its beneficent creative aspect, or the demoniacal goddess Kālī, its evil destructive aspect—two sides of the same supernal coin.

By and large, the West has always believed that reality and the *knowledge* of reality is expressible in mental concepts, and that what cannot be so expressed is fundamentally unreal, that is purely "subjective." The East, on the contrary, believes that reality and the *experience* of it lies beyond the mind (*manas*) and all mental processes, that rational and discursive thought is incapable of apprehending it; furthermore, it believes that it can establish close contact with it, and eventually merge with it, by overcoming mental activity altogether. The West's ultimate goal is to know *about* and relate to the Ultimate Object, the East's is to identify with and *be* the Ultimate Subject. The following parable may help illustrate the contrast: let us imagine a crossroads with one sign on the right pointing "to heaven" and another on the left pointing to "lectures on heaven"; the Easterner would turn right and go straight to heaven, while the Westerner would turn left and attend the lectures.

The West believes that rational thought is the main, if not the sole tool in its search for ultimate reality; the East believes that the whole of consciousness (*dṛk*) is required for this task: consciousness being understood as including, not only the rational mind (*manas*) and the reflective intellect (*tarka*), but also intuition (*buddhi*), perception (*pratyakṣa*) and emotion (*rasa*)—emotion viewed as a fusion or integration of physiological reaction and mental representation. The whole of consciousness is evidently far more extensive than rational thought alone and encompasses it as one of its components. The West strives for the elaboration of autonomous, non-emotional intellectual structures that do *not* involve the other components of consciousness. Such abstract structures are purely cerebral entities derived from logical thought, which can deal as well with the spiritual world as conceived by Western theologies, as with the physical world handled by science. The close connection between Western theologies and scientific thought is perfectly clear, the latter being the natural offspring of the former. It is only an apparent paradox that the Western scientific attitude and mental discipline spring precisely from medieval scholasticism, from the theological gymnastics of such mental giants as Duns Scotus and Abelard who shaped the word-symbol into a tool of almost mathematical precision and made possible the total independence of the abstract idea from aesthetic impression and emotional involvement. Western thought was no longer chained to subjective sensation and could therefore enter into an objective relationship with the world of spirit as well as with the world of physical nature.

We know all about the concrete results of this objective scrutiny of physical nature—the universe that science has uncovered and the world that technology has mastered. Unfortunately, the same intellectual tools could not be applied to the spiritual world without leading to mental bankruptcy. It is a striking fact that whereas the Westerner often believes in the literal truth of his myths, Scriptures and dogmas, and often assumes that their contents are historical *facts*, very much as the Victorian physicist thought that his scientific world-picture literally described the world as it is, the Easterner does nothing of the kind—indeed, has no dogmas at all, sees in all myths merely useful symbolism and does not care at all about historical fact. In the West, there is spiritual ambiguity between "fact" and "symbol"; in the East, there can be no such ambiguity since only the symbol exists—there is no proper "object," therefore there is no fact as such.

The fact does not point beyond itself; the symbol does and functions as a means of transformation, as a transformer of energy. The true root of superstition is taking a symbol for a literal fact. When Bishop Wilberforce, for instance, attacked the concept of Darwinian Evolution, he went out on a superstitious limb, claiming that "the principle of natural selection is absolutely incompatible with the word of God," because if Darwin is right, "Genesis is a lie, the whole framework of the book of life falls to pieces, and the revelation of God to man, as we Christians know it, is a delusion and a snare."[18] This is a perfect example of confusion between fact and symbol, and too many such Western simpletons have been mistaking one for the other for centuries. The root of the pseudo-conflict between science and religion, materialism and spiritualism lies right here, in this ambiguity, and concerns only the West. No such conflict is possible in the East where all mythologies and philosophies are understood to be simply allegorical, implying no literal truth or factual statement whatsoever, and therefore no possibility of collision with a scientific view of the universe.

It does matter a great deal to the West whether Christ rose bodily from the dead, multiplied bread loaves or even existed at all; it does not matter one whit to the East whether Rāma, Śiva or Buddha ever existed since their importance is neither factual nor historical but purely symbolic. No Easterner would think of duplicating Tertullian's comment on Christ's Resurrection—*et sepultus resurrexit, certum est quia impossibile est* (and he was buried and rose again; it is certain because it is impossible)—because in the East there is no conflict between fact and faith, since Eastern faith (*śraddhā*) aims basically at subjective cognition rather than the objective "believing to be true" of the Westerner. The West has always attempted to impose dogmatically its various viewpoints because, imbued with a Biblical, Catholic or Koranic sense of God-given historical mission and the conviction of having the *monopoly* of literal religious truth, it felt that it was objectively in the right—regardless of the increasing conflict, within its own cultures, between the spiritual messages (often mutually contradictory) of its "revealed" religions and scientific knowledge.

In the process, ever since the Greeks, the West's increasing scientific knowledge has outgrown the mythological and theological cocoons from which it sprang and has often violently rejected the ancestral myths and venerable symbolism which nursed its cultural childhood, swinging wildly from literal acceptance to total negation, finally kicking away the mythological ladder whose steps had enabled it to expand its vision in the first place. The Greeks had already done it. When, in the fifth century B.C. Anaxagoras declared the sun to be a mere ball of fire rather than the sun-god Helios—and was banished from Athens for his pains—he symbolized this stark rejection of myth as a valuable instrument of knowledge. Socrates, who had undergone a striking mystical experience at Potidae which changed the course of his life, refused to express faith in the tutelary deities of Athens and was sentenced to drink his deadly cup of hemlock. Greek philosophy finally mocked the Olympian gods out of existence.

The East also expanded its knowledge and cultures but without ever rejecting the mythologies from which they issued; it did not have to, since the subjectifying outlook never took these myths to be anything but metaphorical formulations of higher and deeper truths, that is projected contents of an unconscious mind (*vāsanā*) that was understood and accepted as being closer to ultimate reality than rational thought in the state of waking-consciousness (*jāgaraṇa*). Eastern creeds have generated innumerable gods and goddesses; but they were always conceived by Eastern wisdom as belonging to the illusory realm of *māyā*, to be eventually dismissed and dissolved when consciousness rises to the highest plane (*vijñāna*); and just like the phenomenal-mental world of *māyā* itself (of which they are a product), they *exist* but are fundamentally *unreal*. Eastern myths, unlike their Western counterparts, are not mere poetry; they are essentially channels whereby translogical meaning is conveyed; they are all transrational metaphors and allegories, and are clearly understood to be such by the evolved Easterners—this, in such a way, that there is no sharp discontinuity between the more literal beliefs of the devotional masses and the penetrating understanding of the cultural elite. Mythology and philosophy proceed hand in hand, enriching each other. The gods were understood to be nothing more than masks, symbolic *personae* "through" whom higher truths that transcended them were conveyed.

For thousands of years, the Western mind has made vain efforts to adduce rational proofs of the existence of an objectified God as First Cause, Prime Mover unmoved or *Deus ex Machina*. In Aristotle's philosophy, spiritual monotheism is purely intellectual—the essence of God is "thought directed upon itself. All doing, all willing is directed toward an object distinct from the doer or willer."[19] But, in objectifying the Almighty, the rational mind has, in Dean Inge's words, "to find a place for God in its picture of the world. But God, whose centre is everywhere and His circumference nowhere, cannot be fitted into a diagram. He is rather the canvas on which the picture is painted, or the frame in which it is set."[20] These words from the worthy Dean of St. Paul's come much closer to describing the monistic outlook of the East than Western monotheism. To this day, all purely intellectual attempts to prove the existence of an objectified God have failed.

The East, early on, turned its back on this relentless pursuit of the Supreme Object by focusing on the Supreme Subject, that is on the "canvas" on which the objective picture is projected. As a result of these divergent aims, whereas Western philosophies are mental disciplines of strict intellectual *information*, Eastern philosophies are methods of total *transformation*. To the Easterner, religion is an awareness of ultimate reality, not an intellectual theory about it; it is psychology and method rather than theology and dogma. So that while the Westerner advances from thought to thought, from abstract concept to abstract concept, deducing, inducing, analyzing, synthesizing, the Easterner advances from one subjective condition to another. The Westerner delves deeper and deeper into the realm of pure cerebral abstraction, from particular to general concepts, from experimental work to scientific knowledge of the objective world, while the Easterner changes ceaselessly his states of consciousness (*cittavṛtti*). The Westerner focuses on the *objects* of rational thought, the Easterner on consciousness devoid of objective contents: Eastern philosophies are basically empirical descriptions of the possible evolution of man from one level of consciousness to higher ones. To sum up, the Westerner aims at clear *thought*, the Easterner at pure *consciousness* with no objects in sight, *ālaya-vijñana* in Buddhist terminology, which is practically synonymous with *śūnya*, the "Void."

The main weapon in the intellectual arsenal of the West is the law of causality which, strictly speaking, has no true application in Eastern consciousness because the cause and effect sequence involves a notion of succession in linear time—by definition, an efficient cause always precedes its effect—which means nothing to a form of consciousness that ignores linear time and focuses on the timeless. It is, for instance, highly symbolic that, to this day, the Hindi word *kal* signifies both "yesterday" and "tomorrow"; what kind of causal sequence could be fitted in this psychological and linguistic context? Even the Buddhist "Law of Karma," incorrectly interpreted as the "Chain of Causation," which regulates the round of births and rebirths, bears only the slightest resemblance to causality since the whole process of reincarnation takes place *outside* of time, not within it. Furthermore, causality is a purely mechanical relationship based on an intellectual concept; *karma*, on the other hand, is an *organic* life-process generating reincarnation.[21] Instead of cause and effect, we have "origination" (*utpāda*), "growth" (*jarā*) and "destruction" (*nirodha*), regulating this organic development from birth, youth, adolescence through adulthood to old age and death, applied to the whole round of births and rebirths.[22] The karmic procreative urges that survive death and dwell beyond time and space longing for rebirth in space–time, are not causes but organic "germs"—and they are no more the causes of rebirth than a seed is the "cause" of the plant that grows out of it: "Karma is the universal 'seed' (*bīja*) of which all action is the fruit,"[23] which is fundamentally a law of the conservation of moral energy: "We reap what we sow," in this life or in another.

This Eastern outlook is a highly sophisticated form of sympathetic magic based on the concept that like attracts like, that when there is X, there is automatically Y—a timeless congruence between two entities, not a time-based sequence of cause and effect. The East focuses on the realm of nature, the endless pulsation of life based on the recurrence of the tides, the seasons, sunrise and sunset—everywhere, there is meaningful coordination and concurrence in which the natural evolution of karmic urges finds its rightful place. In the Eastern view, the only valid aim is, not to break through intellectually with the mind in order to overpower nature, in the Western fashion, but to overcome the natural pulsation of endless life and eventually get out of the universal rhythm altogether by annihilating the karmic urges themselves: the goal of the *yogī*.

The Western mind, in contrast, is forever shifting between two widely divergent poles: assertion of power and control over the object, along with the inevitable submission to the objective data it is manipulating. Eastern consciousness, inherently serene and calm, dismisses this strenuous and shifting struggle since it ignores the autonomy or even the fundamental reality of the non-subject; it looks upon the phenomenal world of matter (*prakṛti*) as corresponding structurally to the rational mind (*manas*) that apprehends it as if it were made for it and which shares in its degree of unreality—therefore, both mental activity and the external material world, if they are to disappear, must disappear together. In other words, the primacy of the Self remains unimpaired and the phenomenal world of sense-perceptions, which is suspended to the mind, ultimately disappears when mental activity itself is overcome and movement from thought to thought ceases altogether: Patañjali defines the aim of Yoga as the "suppression of the spontaneous activities of the mind-stuff" (*yogaś cittavṛtti-nirodhyaḥ*).[24]

Long before the goal is in sight, however, the striving Easterner reaches a point of spiritual self-sufficiency and self-possession that generates an atmosphere of superior calm, equanimity and serenity; he dwells in himself as if it were a universe of its own, the only real one into which, gradually, all the elements of the external, illusory realm of *māyā* are absorbed and dissolved. Supremacy of the Self inevitably entails an attitude of timeless remoteness which strikes the Westerner as fatalistic passivity but is nothing of the kind. This internal universe itself, so long as it is not purified, is replete with non-subjective elements such as random thoughts (*sarvārthatā*) standing in the way of the realization of the Self; elements that have to be disciplined and brought under control before they can be dismissed as illusory.

The ultimate goal of Eastern Self-realization is provided by the hallowed Indian expression, *tat tvam asi*, "That Thou Art," the principle of the fundamental identity of the Self (*ātman*) and Brahman, which is reached at the end of the mystical or yogic "way." This is no longer theoretical knowledge; this transformational goal can only be reached by concentration and meditation and the overcoming of all mental processes, assisted by appropriate psychosomatic techniques (*askesis*) aimed at dismantling all the obstacles standing in the way.

The *Bhagavad Gītā* gives us a perfect example of this predominance of the subjective outlook. This stupendous "Song of the Blessed" depicts the battlefield of Kurukṣetra where two armies stand face to face on the eve of the battle. Arjuna, one of the commanders, drives his war chariot between the lines and, horrified at the thought of the forthcoming slaughter, wants to call off the battle. Lord Kṛṣṇa, the "Mighty One," who assumes temporarily the role of charioteer and incarnates Transcendental Wisdom, urges him to fight regardless of the "objective" consequences, and his speech is the essence of the *Gita*'s message: Arjuna must fight with serenity and total detachment because it is his duty as a professional warrior, because he is bound by the *karma* of his past and has to go inexorably through the mysterious labyrinth of his appointed duties, however evil the consequences may seem to others. Since actions have no objective value, his sole duty is to consider his own subjective state, not the objective result of his actions, such as the massacre he is about to start and which is the *sole concern of his victims*. The Mighty One emphasizes the point by saying to Arjuna: "You sorrow for men who do not need your sorrow ... Wise men do not sorrow for the living or the dead [25] ... Long since have these men in truth been slain by Me; yours is to be the mere occasion ... Slay them then—why falter?" [26] Lord Kṛṣṇa then adds: "Consider pleasure and pain, wealth and poverty, victory and defeat, as of equal worth. Prepare for the combat. Acting in this way thou wilt not become stained by guilt." [27]

The immediate message: there is no such a thing as objective reality. And the ultimate message: "Give thought to nothing but the act, renounce its fruits (*phalatṛṣṇavairāgya*) ... For him who achieves inward detachment (*tyāgin*), neither good nor evil exists any longer here below (*vigatakalmaṣaḥ*)." [28] We are far, here, from Christian charity and love!

The roots of this subjectifying attitude go far back and eliminate the typical ethical framework in which objectifying cultures and societies live; while Brahman (and, consequently, *ātman*) is *beyond* good and evil, Yahweh, God or Allah *are* goodness itself as opposed to Satan or the Evil One. For instance, in the *Kauṣītakī Upaniṣad*, the god Indra, incarnating the Absolute, boasts of his apparently wicked deeds and then addresses his worshipper: "Understand me as I am ... with one who knows me, his world is injured by no deed whatsoever, not by the murder of his father, not by the murder of his mother, not by theft, not by the slaughter of an embryo. Whatever evil he does, he does not blanch."[29] We also read in the *Bṛhadaranyaka Upaniṣad*: "He does not become greater by good action nor inferior by bad action."[30]

Western love, charity and ethics, in contrast, are the fruit of an outlook based on the absolute dissociation of every individual human being from every other, and the equally sharp dissociation of all human beings from God Almighty. Love implies *tension* between distinct entities, between man and God, "I" and "thou," and it can exist in the East only to the extent that such distinctions are maintained as they are in the *bhakti* variety of Indian religiosity—that is, resting at the stage preliminary to actual identification between *ātman* and Brahman. Furthermore, there was in the West, until the advent of psychoanalysis and depth psychology, no conscious problem of self-identification, no probing of one's deeper layers of the unconscious; the Western problem was how to relate to a Divine power outside oneself and how to develop one's original and unique "personality" (*asmitā*, which must be eliminated in the East), that is one's ego—and love characterizes a relation between distinct individual egos or, at its best, between ego and an objectified and personalized God. In the East, the problem is to overcome and extinguish the ego as an essential step on the way to the discovery of one's fundamental identity with the divine within, and to the discovery of the basic unity and one-ness of all things and beings. Śrī Rāmakrishna gives us a pun-gent pictorial image of the problem as seen from the Eastern standpoint: "Think of a vast ocean filled with water on all sides. A jar is immersed in it. There is water both inside and outside the jar; but the water does not become one un-less the jar is broken[31] . . . What is the jar? It is I-conscious-ness (ego). When the I disappears, what *is* remains."[32]

In the Eastern context, we have "compassion" (*karuṇā*) or "benevolence" (*jen*) in China, instead of love (*prema*), compassion for the suffering of others who, after all, are also ourselves; compassion is what Arjuna feels for his future victims, even though he has to go through with his appointed earthly duties at their expense. In fact, the greatest praise bestowed by the *Gītā* is on those who share in others' pains and sorrows as their very own.[33] Of course, from the Western standpoint, there is a certain icy coldness in the Eastern detachment (*tyāgin*), which comes through quite clearly in the following statement of the *Gītā*'s Lord Kṛṣṇa: "In all contingent beings the same am I; none do I hate and none do I fondly love."[34]

Mysticism is the same phenomenon the world over, in the East as in the West; but whereas the East bases its metaphysical insights upon it, the West has refused to do so. If we study the records and descriptions left to us by all the mystics of the world, we are struck by a universal insist-ence on the fact that all distinction between things, men, object and subject, is overcome and abolished—the world becomes "One," which is the essence of the monistic philo-sophy of India's Vedānta school as expounded by the great Śaṇkara, its foremost mystic–philosopher. This, the West-ern intellect resists with all its might since it destroys the essential monotheistic idea of a sharp distinction between man and God, between creature and Creator; it makes a mockery of the idea that the course of human history has a spiritual meaning; and it abolishes all the analytical claims of Western thought as to the sharp opposition between subject and object. No wonder that Western mystics have always had to contend with the underlying hostility of the cultural environment into which they were born. Even Islam had to put to death the great mystic al-Ḥallāj for having had the audacity to claim blasphemously that he had become God (*Anā'l-Ḥaqq*, "I am the Truth," that is to say "I am God"). Thereafter, all Muslim mystics prudently stated that mystical insight (*fanā*) implied neither the extinction of the personality nor any merger with Allah.

The German mystic Meister Eckhart did feel that he had become divine, and Pope John XXII condemned him for teaching that man and God shared a common divinity; his trial in Avignon was aborted by his untimely death; while Suso, another of the great German mystics, cautiously refrained from following in his footsteps because of this dogmatic hostility. And unless honest enough to claim, like Aquinas, that their intellectual work was "straw" compared with the true mystical experience, they had to go through extraordinary contortions in order to avoid a headlong clash with the Church (or the *ulamās*, in the case of Islam): as St. John of the Cross put it in his *Dark Night of the Soul*, "I trust neither to experience nor to knowledge ... but solely to the Holy Scriptures ... it is not my intention to depart from the sound doctrine of our holy mother the Catholic Church. I resign myself absolutely to her light, and submit to her decisions."[35] In other words, total surrender to the dogmatic discipline of the Church.

In the East there can be such surrender since the philosophical premises that make such a capitulation necessary in the West do not exist—it is acknowledged in the Orient that ultimate reality is precisely what the mystic experiences, and that this experience is the actual recovery of his inner, divine Self; he becomes, in fact, what he has actually always been behind the veil of *māyā*. Whereas, time and again, the Western mystic is warned not to let himself be carried away by the subjective "illusion" of his own potential divinity, warned that there can be no divine incarnation in man— save in the one and only case of Jesus for the Christians— and that his rapturous experience is actually a "vision" of an objectified, transcendent and forever separate Almighty God, rather than a "fusion" with It.

In spite of all these strictures, Western mystics managed often enough to convey the essence of their ecstasies which agrees, by and large, with the Eastern testimonies: the essence is the monistic feeling that "all is one," that the seer and the seen are identical, that there is no division or distinction between one thing and another; the corollary is that the experience completely transcends the rational mind and that it is therefore literally ineffable; and finally that this experience is an overwhelmingly emotional one, involving supreme peace "that passes all understanding," total calm and total blessedness. As the pagan mystic–philosopher Plotinus put it: "The man is changed, no longer himself, nor self-belonging; he is merged with the Supreme, sunken into It, one with It ... This is why the vision baffles telling; for how could a man bring back tidings of the Supreme as detached when he has seen It as one with himself?" [36]

It is interesting to note that the same Plotinus had enrolled in the Roman army of Emperor Gordian in the hope of reaching Persia and India in order to study Eastern wisdom at first hand [37]—a logical attempt, although unsuccessful, on the part of a mystic who felt that the human soul was in fact *pars divinae substantiae*. [38] Plotinus' monistic doctrine was the main metaphysical challenge to the early Christian theology and represented that Neoplatonic and Gnostic trend in the first centuries A.D. that came close to the Oriental outlook—hence, its ultimate demise in the West because it was entirely based on an unchallenged mystical insight which actually experiences the One. The heirs of Greek culture and Hebrew tradition would not accept the validity of that experience. As Erwin Schrödinger tells us, "The multiplicity is only apparent. This is the doctrine of the *Upaniṣads*. And not of the *Upaniṣads* only. The mystical experience of the union with God regularly leads to this view, unless strong prejudices stand in its way, and therefore, more easily in the East than in the West." And he quotes the Persian mystic Aẕiz Nasafī who claimed that,

> At the death of every living being the spirit returns to the world of spirits and the body to the world of bodies. But only the bodies change in the process. The world of spirits is a single spirit standing like a light in back of the world of bodies and shining through each individual that comes into existence as through a window. According to the kind and size of the window, more or less light penetrates into the world. But the light always remains the same.[39]

The true mystical experience is in complete contradiction with the main trend of the Western philosophic tradition; no wonder that time and again, the objectifying, analytical mind of the West has viewed mysticism, either with distrust, or as sheer delusion or superstition. Whereas the East views precisely this objectifying, analytical mind as the source of all delusions; as the Buddhist philosopher Aśvaghoṣa put it, "As soon as the mind perceives differences, it awakens desire, grasping and ... suffering, and then the mind notes that some relate to himself and some to not-Self. If the mind could remain undisturbed by differences and discriminations, the concept of an ego (the root of moral evil) would die away."[40]

In *early* Buddhism, we reach the height of total subjectivity untainted by any attempt, even temporary, at objectification: Buddha refuses to discuss the reality of Brahman or *ātman*, merely stressing the sole reality of *nirvāṇa*, the subjective state of mystical enlightenment—which has brought upon him the accusation of atheism; but this accusation is totally *irrelevant* to the extent that early Buddhism was simply not interested in any kind of objectification whatsoever. Early Buddhism, unlike Hinduism, displays no encyclopaedic theory of the cosmos, sees no permanent Self in man or beyond, no Brahman, entertains no metaphysical and ontological propositions concerning man or the universe; it is pure and simple depth psychology in the proper, non-Western sense of the term. All striving is focused on the actual realization of the subject and its release (*mokṣa*) from the fetters of the phenomenal world of time and space. Buddha merely posits the total unreality of any stable substance or mental concept—*sarvam dukham, sarvam anityam*, "all is painful, all is transient," claiming that everything is in a perpetual flux, that only events take place—reminding us of Alfred North Whitehead's summing up of his philosophy of science: "The event is the unit of things real."

Buddha attacked all those who claimed that they could define Brahman or *ātman* or assert their existence or even non-existence: "To maintain that the *ātman* exists, real, permanent, is a false view; to maintain that it does not exist is a false view."[41] All problems and all solutions are within the subject; as Buddha put it, "It is in the fathom-long carcass, friend, with its impressions and ideas that, I declare, lies the world, and the root of the world, and the cessation of the world, and the course of action that leads to the cessation of the world."[42] The same interpretation is valid for the other so-called "atheistic" schools of Eastern philosophy such as Sāṃkhya and Yoga in which total subjectivity prevails—the real is solely what you *experience*, not what you think. All attempts at identifying and defining the Supreme Reality, God, Allah, Yahweh, Brahman, are pointless and meaningless verbalizations since they all hint at some ultimate reality that is beyond time and space as well as life and death, that is literally ineffable—and yet can, surprisingly, be actually experienced by man—seen by the "eye of the saints" (*ariya cakku*) as the Buddhists put it, that is by the transcendent "eye" of Bodhic insight that sees beyond the phenomenal world—the "Eye of Śiva," that is the eye of pure consciousness in Hinduism.

4 SQUARING THE CIRCLE: BEYOND THE MIND

According to Plutarch, Alexander the Great, shortly after entering the mysterious land of India from Afghanistan, came unexpectedly upon a party of *digambaras*, naked philosopher-saints of the Jain persuasion who became known to the amazed Greeks and Macedonians (*yavanas*, to the Indians) as "gymnosophists," *hylobiói*. These naked ascetics, sitting on the outskirts of the great university city of Takṣaśilā (Taxila), practised austerities that astounded the Greeks. Pricked by a curiosity aroused by their local fame and prestige, Alexander proceeded to put to them a number of insoluble questions, threatening to have those who gave him the worst answers put to death; but so thrilled was he by their subtle replies that he sent them away loaded with gifts. And although most Greek intellectuals accompanying his army complained that trying to understand Indian philosophy was like "making water flow through mud,"[1] he asked the Greek philosopher Onesicritus, a disciple of Diogenes the Cynic, to seek out the greatest holy men; brought into the presence of the celebrated Jain saint Kalyāna (Kalanos, in Greek), he was treated by him with the greatest "insolence" and ordered to strip off his clothes and stand stark naked. The tale does not relate Onesicritus' answer but the upshot was that Alexander took Kalyāna as his *guru* in replacement of his boyhood tutor, Aristotle, and brought him back with him to Babylon.[2]

If Aristotle heard about it, back in distant Greece, he

must have been amazed. Aristotle despised all "barbarians" and strongly disapproved of treating them on an equal footing with Greeks. He could not have foreseen that this episode symbolized the first baffling encounter between East and West, nor the centuries of close contacts between Greeks—often as Hellenistic ambassadors to Indian courts, then as rulers and artists in Bactria—and Indians. Many Greeks fell under the spell of Hindu or Buddhist philosophies and life-styles. We know, for instance, that Pyrrho of Elis, who founded the philosophic school of "pure scepticism" (Pyrrhonism) in Greece around 330 B.C. joined Alexander's expedition to India and was strongly influenced by the various *saddhus* he encountered and by that serene indifference to external circumstances for which Greek philosophers yearned but almost never achieved. According to Philostratus, Apollonius of Tyana claimed that "All wish to live in the nearness of God, but only the Hindus bring it to pass." [3] The historical record, however, shows no reciprocity; no Indian seemed to have been impressed or influenced by Greek philosophical speculations. And when such contacts eventually came to an end, little interpenetration had occurred: East remained East and West remained West; and the philosophic evolution of the West was going to be shaped, in large part, by Aristotle.

Around the time of Alexander's penetration into India, Aristotle was indeed brilliantly concluding the main phase of Greek philosophical thinking by putting a capstone on it. He was then the esteemed founder of the science of logic; his *Organon*, translated by Boethius in the sixth century A.D., became the straitjacket that imprisoned Western philosophical and theological thought for millennia. It is from Aristotle on that, with some exceptions, the Western trend toward objectification proceeded unhindered and untroubled by any remote influence from the East; and that knowledge of ultimate reality was presumed to be the prerogative of reason and logic. His concept of a rational soul was "pure thought" since only abstract thought was immortal, and his objectified God coincided with the proper functioning of efficient causality—the Almighty was defined the "Prime Mover Unmoved" (*primum mobile immotum*) and was the only entity that was pure "form" without matter. He put "mind" above "soul"; the timeless mind was that which understands philosophy and mathematics, and is therefore immortal—whereas the soul is what moves the body, causes sensations, nutrition, feeling, and is inevitably as perishable as the body. It is only later, with the advent of the concept of "personality" (a restriction and a characteristic of the finite for the Greeks as it was for the Easterners) through the ministrations of Christianity that the imperishable soul individually existent beyond death came into the Western picture. At any rate, it is thanks to Aristotle that the Western mind was firmly set on its objectifying course for many centuries. What might have happened if he had accompanied his former pupil Alexander to India?

In order to fully grasp the fundamental difference between the Eastern and Western approaches to metaphysics, let us revert for a while to the distant days of prehistory before the magic world-outlook dissolved under the impact of rational thinking like early morning mist under the rays of the rising sun. During hundreds of thousands of years of man's early evolution, man lived essentially as a problem-solving, tool-making being. Quite naturally, his evolving intellect developed in an essentially practical direction, intent upon enhancing the quality of life, basically geared to *action* on the environment rather than theoretical abstractions. Needless to say, human language was shaped in such a way as to assist action rather than thought. Anthropologist Bronislaw Malinovsky points out: "We have to realize that language, originally, was never used as a mere mirror of reflected thought ... In its primitive uses, language functions as a link in concerted human activity, as a piece of human behaviour. It is a mode of action and not an instrument of reflection."[4] And he adds further: "This perspective has allowed us to class human speech with the active modes of human behaviour, rather than with the reflective and cognitive ones."[5] In short, he sharply distinguishes between "modes of action" and "means of thinking."

Man's developing intellect was therefore shaped by the vital need to act on his physical environment—*primum vivere, deinde philosophari,* one must live before one can philosophize. This practical bent of man's evolving mind implies that rational thought is at ease with the material world, aims at controlling physical phenomena and at guiding the human body's contacts with the natural environment. Being atavistically conditioned to utilize material things, rational thought partakes of matter's structure; but being created to understand one part of reality, it cannot possibly pretend to understand the whole. In prehistoric times, thinking was entirely subordinate to living, to solving hunting problems, to tool-making. In this endeavour, the developing rational thought's utilitarian bent adapted its structure to the material world, in effect leaving intuition to deal with the inner life; quite clearly, the habits formed by the need for action on the environment have influenced *abstract* thought and distorted it, creating thereby false problems that have to be dismissed by metaphysics. As Miguel de Unamuno put it in his *Tragic Sense of Life,* "Everything vital is anti-rational, not merely irrational, and everything rational is anti-vital."[6]

The Second Law of Thermodynamics indicates, in brief, that heat, left to its own devices, will always flow from higher to lower temperatures, which implies that inorganic matter tends to become increasingly disorderly and therefore more and more random in nature: in effect, the material universe tends to run down. Moving against this trend, Evolution shows that living matter moves progressively toward the spontaneous creation of increasingly complex organisms endowed with increasingly higher levels of organization. This implies that life is an effort to climb the slope that inorganic matter descends: matter moves ceaselessly toward a state of disorganization, life toward increasingly complex forms of purposeful organization. It was therefore inevitable that Western man's objectifying mind split into two sharply separated components in order to assert its mastery over the external environment: his rational and analytical mind inserted itself deeply into the physical world, adapting itself to the inner structure of matter as apprehended by the senses, turning its back on life and vitality; while the rest of his consciousness, his intuition and his unconscious went on marching in the opposite direction, that is the same direction as that of life itself. It is out of this growing schizophrenia that all the philosophical problems of the West have sprung. We must again listen to Unamuno's passionate exposition on this theme because it epitomizes the West's metaphysical dilemma:

> The mind seeks what is dead, for what is living escapes it; it seeks to congeal the flowing stream in blocks of ice; it seeks to arrest it. In order to analyze a body, it is necessary to extenuate or destroy it. In order to understand anything it is necessary to kill it, to lay it out rigid in the mind. Science is a cemetery of dead ideas, even though life may issue from them. Worms also feed upon corpses. How, then, shall reason open its portals to the revelation of life? It is a tragic combat—it is the very essence of tragedy—this combat of life with reason . . . The rational, in effect, is simply the relational; reason is limited to relating irrational elements.[7]

Is that not, to a certain extent, what contemporary physics are telling us? The essential point, here, is that the conscious, rational intellect is essentially a *blocking* mechanism, intended to bring up to the level of waking-consciousness *only* those thoughts that are practically useful in helping the living process at a given moment; everything else is shoved back into the unconscious where it becomes part of the stuff that dreams are made of, the essential constituents of the subject himself. This is exactly where the iron curtain is rung down in the West: between the conscious mind and the unconscious, between the objective and the subjective. And this is why the process of getting *beyond* the conscious mind and silencing its activities is the primary goal of those who seek to know and realize the deep Self.

Western speculative philosophy therefore embarked on its rational and logical career, using for metaphysical purposes a discursive intellect that had not been devised for them. While Eastern consciousness soon realized that this was so, Western philosophy did not. Rational and logical thought cannot apprehend life itself since it is a continuous flow of unrepeatable events which only intuition can grasp. Rational thought, to paraphrase Henri Bergson's famous metaphor, proceeds like the cinema, in that it attempts to understand motion and "becoming" by describing it from the outside as a succession of stationary states—as the pioneering statement of the Greek Eleatic school on Zeno's arrow clearly demonstrates. In fact, there is more to the process of becoming than a series of static positions which rational thought obtains by cutting motionless sections out of motion. The notion of becoming simply goes against the grain of rational thought and language. Becoming is an undeniable fact, but rational thought seeks to find, below evolutive becoming, what is changeless and lifeless. This is what led straight to Plato's philosophy of Ideas; this is how the Greeks mistook the appearance created by the rational mind for the real. Instead of looking upon objectified ideas as artificial cuttings sliced out of becoming, they saw in them the actual building blocks of objective reality. The inevitable outcome was, of course, Aristotelian logic with its rigid laws of identity, contradiction and the excluded middle which has been blamed in modern times for hindering the development of scientific thought; as we know today, contemporary physics gives us an apparently paradoxical but definitely non-Aristotelian picture of physical reality.

The conceptual network created by Western rational thought thus became more real to the West than the mysterious and ever-evolving world of life and consciousness. The great intellectual structure created by conscious and rational thought finally proved incapable of coming to grips with what was bound to elude it—the endless becoming in which life and consciousness evolve. Ever since the Greeks, Western philosophical thought has remained under the spell of mathematics and has been hardly more than a systematization of physical science. Even in Spinoza and Leibnitz, one can see that the skeletons of their doctrines are Platonism and Aristotelism, refracted through the Cartesian mechanistic outlook, and this in spite of their undoubted originality.

The outcome of this secular trend is the dilemma in which Western metaphysical thought now finds itself. Scientific thought must operate as if its method's efficiency had no limits—even if, later on, it must come to the conclusion that such limitations exist, as is the case in contemporary physics. But the philosophical temptation to hypostatize this scientific thrust—which is purely methodological for the scientists—and convert what is merely a useful method into a fundamental law of all things proved too great to be resisted. This is why, until recently, Western thought looked upon the universe as a cosmic machine, ruled by the iron mathematical *laws* that came to replace the abstract *concepts* of Greek philosophy; it still remains that the modern Western outlook remained a mere transposition of the defective Greek metaphysics. The fact that some of the new physicists of the twentieth century now claim that the universe looks increasingly like a great "thought" rather than a machine implies a certain degree of emancipation from the mechanistic model; but what they really mean is that the universe looks increasingly like a cosmic "consciousness" rather than a great "thought," since machines are, anyway, a pure product of rational thought and both twins are children of the Western tendency to objectify endlessly until the ultimate object is reached. In this context, the ultimate object can only be thought thinking itself, very much like Aristotle's God (the thought of thought) or Hegel's Absolute: the real, the Absolute is thought.[8]

Thought thinking itself, however, is also the ultimate absurdity; and soon enough, the Western intellect had to come to the conclusion that ultimate reality is simply ungraspable. That was, more or less, Kant's position: the intellect can deal with the world of the phenomenon but not with the reality underlying it, the mysterious background or substratum of the *noumenon*, the "thing-in-itself." He asserted that a part of knowledge is extra-intellectual but refused to deal with this *a priori*, claiming that the framework of understanding must be accepted as it is, ready-made. Kant, however, overlooked the fact that logical thought and creative experience move in two contrary directions—one, according to the rational intellect which, geared to act on the objective world of matter and partaking of its structure, descends toward it and turns its back on life; the other, moving in the same direction as life, involves the whole of consciousness with its intuitive component. Kant thought of intuition as being *infra*-intellectual—typical of the Western approach—whereas in fact it is *supra*-intellectual, overflowing and surrounding on all sides the narrow limits of the rational mind as the iris of the eye surrounds the pupil: this is the fundamental discovery of Eastern thought. The *Bhagavad Gītā* states plainly that "The sense-perceptions (*indriyān*) are superior to the physical body (*sthūla*); the mind (*manas*) is superior to the senses; intuitive understanding (*buddhi*) again is superior to the mind." And it adds, of course, that "superior to intuitive understanding is He, the Self." [9]

It is interesting to note that neurophysiology now tells us that the two hemispheres of the brain each specialize in different functions of cognition—the left dedicating itself to logical and analytical thinking, seat of verbal thought; the right to intuition and holistic understanding of patterns, with an ability to grasp directly the relationship between parts of a whole. One operates linguistically with rational sequences of deductions and inductions; the other intuitively juxtaposes images and symbols, integrates and synthesizes rather than analyses. [10] It seems obvious that Western philosophic and scientific culture has, so to speak, atrophied the right hemisphere of the brain, while Eastern cultures have given it predominance—or rather, it might well be the other way around in the sense that the cultural divergence between East and West would have its origin in a physiological differentiation in the brain.

The proper role of metaphysics is therefore to use the whole of consciousness with its intuitive component in order to insert itself in the living evolutionary movement of *becoming* instead of recreating it artificially with the dead fragments of itself. Without formulating it thus, this is what Eastern thought aimed at—which is why, thanks to its subjectifying outlook, it was able to see that metaphysics should be one of *transformation*, striving to achieve a coincidence of individual consciousness with the living principle that generates it. Western philosophical thought never knew, until Henri Bergson's *Creative Evolution*, what to do with intuition (although it acknowledged its existence and used it freely) because it is precisely in this kind of insight that object and subject coincide and merge—and this is also precisely what Western analytical and objectifying thought refuses to accept.

For the objectifying mind, transformation is far more difficult than intellectual *information*. When objectifying the mental world of ideas and concepts as well as the physical world of matter, the Western mind was compelled to turn its back on the world of inner experience, the same world that becomes the proper terrain for the exertions of the Eastern mind. In this intuitive approach which involves the whole of consciousness, the Easterner reaches direct understanding and realization; the Western philosopher, using his abstract rationalism, can give us only skeletal metaphors; it was and is easier for him to use ideas and concepts placed in advance in language as if, brought down from heaven, they revealed elements of ultimate reality. But, as an old Chinese saying expresses it, "The treasures (cognition) of the house (intuition) do not come in through the gate (intellect)." [11]

It is evident that the fatal weakness of Western philosophies, theologies and metaphysics is that they developed, unlike the sciences of nature, *outside* the field of experience, in a world of pure mental concepts disconnected from reality. The Western God, supreme concept for some, Absolute Object of the theologian, was *de facto* disconnected from the emotional God of religion which was always felt, especially by Western mystics, to be pure Subject. An objectified Almighty is an abstract idea, not a living reality; purely verbal, empty of contents, a meaningless sign. And the same goes for all the other modern substitutes for God; whenever terminology designates the ultimate concept as Kant's "thing-in-itself," Spinoza's "substance," Hegel's "idea," Marx's "matter," or Schopenhauer's "will," we are left with nothing but empty verbalization. Once a substitute is applied and extended to everything, to ultimate reality, it loses all significance. Take Schopenhauer's "will," for instance: will is that which is opposed to non-will; how then can matter be different from spirit if both are, ultimately, will? To put "will" or "matter" everywhere amounts to putting it nowhere.

The great error of Western thought is to believe that it

knows something about ultimate reality by giving it a name; word-coinage, however, is no solution. A great extension of meaning entails an ultimate dilution and eventual evaporation of meaning. What advantage is there in saying that the world is "will" or "matter" instead of simply stating that it *is*? What the East has understood far better than the West is that an *existence* can only be given by an *experience*, be it external perception when dealing with the physical world, or intuition when dealing with the inner world of consciousness. Intuition rids us of concepts manufactured by social organisms for practical tasks that have nothing to do with metaphysical insight, which are cut out of the flux of living reality for convenience's sake but which are not connected with experimental reality as lived by consciousness itself.

The obvious conclusion is that the strictly rational mind of waking-consciousness must be *stilled* and then *overcome* before any true metaphysical understanding can be reached.

The primary data that strikes consciousness presents itself in the shape of a fundamental pair of opposites, space and time, which conditions many of the other basic pairs-of-opposites: succession and simultaneity, quality and quantity, homogeneity and heterogeneity, duration and extension. Any culture dedicated to objectification tends to apply a mathematical mind that will emphasize the homogeneous, the quantitative and the extensive, rather than the heterogeneous, the qualitative and the enduring, which are given predominance by the subjectifying cultures of the East. If we start with space, for instance, it is obvious that we must make a sharp distinction between our actual concrete *perception* of extension and our abstract *conception* of space. For theoretical reasons, the Western mind conceived of a completely homogeneous space, that is space without qualities or contents (now overthrown by modern physics); such a notion of space was unknown to magic man, and is unknown to animals for whom space is emphatically *not* homogeneous; and it remained equally alien to the Eastern mind.

But the Western intellect went further and also granted time a similar homogeneity, cutting it up into equal and equivalent slices with its clocks. This kind of time, however, is not time as consciousness lives it but as the rational intellect conceives it in the abstract for practical purposes. What the Western mind has done, in fact, is simply to objectify time by *spatializing* it, reducing it to a dimension of space—a psychological anticipation of Einstein's Relativity; and thanks to Relativity, physics now admits as much: "The fact is that time has become associated with space in physics simply because we have chosen to measure time in terms of space measurements."[12] From then on, the major distinction between time and space will be that space proper is the domain of instantaneous coexistence and time that of succession. As for the time lived by the subject, we will call it *duration*, following Henri Bergson's lead.

From the very start, the objectifying mind of the West confused spatial time with psychological duration, or rather attempted to reduce duration to spatial time. The plain fact, however, is that mutual *exteriority* characterizes elements in space as well as in spatial time; whereas mental states are not exterior to one another when we let ourselves live. A succession of mental states implies mutual *interpenetration* of elements derived from both sense-perceptions and memories of the past. We slice up this interpenetration by juxtaposing a particular thought and a particular external perception, and then isolate the artificial entity thus created. We therefore arbitrarily spatialize duration, which is essentially qualitative and heterogeneous, into quantitative time that is homogeneous and measurable, and project it back into the mind. In the depths of consciousness, however, there is succession without mutual externality; outside, there is mutual externality without succession, a perpetual timeless present, simultaneity; a succession of external moments exists only for a mind that *remembers* them.

Cultures oriented toward the predominance of the subjective will tend to emphasize the heterogeneous and the qualitative, while those that objectify will emphasize the homogeneous and the quantitative. The objectifying Greeks, for instance, dedicated as they were to Euclidean geometry, attributed three characteristics to real space: continuity, homogeneity and isotropism. The subjectifying Chinese, on the other hand, had no conception of abstract, homogeneous space and time. On the contrary, they viewed time as an heterogeneous accumulation of eras, epochs and seasons, space as a group of locations, domains and orientations. They did have generic names for these dimensions: time, in the sense of duration was *chiu* and space, as extension, was *yü*; but the Mohists, for instance, emphasized that they both included multitudes of particular times (*shih*) and spatial locations (*so*) to which they gave priority in the practical arrangements of daily living.[13] As a residue of the magic mind, they sought to remain in tune with the cosmic rhythm and control the times and spaces through their symbolic reproductions in temples and gardens with the assistance of elaborate rites and music.

The remarkable feature of this outlook is that the heterogeneous nature of space, as conceived by the Chinese, resulted in its presumed annihilation where there was no human life while, on the contrary, giving it a maximum of density in the hallowed precinct of the Emperor's palace and temple, the sacred centre of civilization. Space was therefore viewed as a number of spaces or locations distributed according to fixed hierarchy and time as a number of limited cycles and temporal phases. All of them revolved around the imperial Son of Heaven and acquired the maximum of their respective densities *in* the capital city of the civilized world, and *when* the great celebrations and festivities marking the solstices and equinoxes took place. The Son of Heaven lived in pure, unpolluted space, the focus of all the converging attributes. He had to travel around the empire every five years and regulate his majestic progression so as to find himself in the east during the vernal equinox, in the south during the summer solstice, in the west when autumn came and in the north during winter. Space acquired all its proper density around the Emperor and gradually vanished into nought on the periphery of civilization, that is on the borders of the empire. Time was just as much limited by this concept of relativity as space and was organized into a number of definite, closed, discontinuous and unrelated cycles.

And so, the Son of Heaven went about his business of welding the various spaces to the various times, setting the boundaries of contemporary space every five years and marking its emanating centre during the next four. Condensing the spaces into "pure," integral space around him, the Emperor condensed pure time with the help of official celebrations. The small density of time during the dead summer months of hard work without social life gradually increased during the autumn to reach its peak during the ritual jubilees, and it was the Son of Heaven's sacred duty to thus endow, at a given moment and according to the proper etiquette, time and space with their maximum intensity. Such was the outlook of the subjectifying form of consciousness in a great civilization, an external ordering of things that was far truer to man's inner psychological life than any devised by Western cultures.[14] Not only that; even in a certain "objective" way, this outlook anticipated the outlook of Relativity physics. Joseph Needham points it out:

> The assumption underlying the paradoxes would therefore be that within the universal space–time continuum there are an infinitely large number of particular locations

and particular times constantly changing their positions with regard to one another. From the standpoint of an observer at any one of them, the universe will look very different from that which another observer sees. All the paradoxes so far considered fit without difficulty into this scheme. Its striking modernity . . . invites one to wonder what Chinese science would have been capable of, without having to pass through the discipline of Aristotelian logic . . .[15]

The rise of Western philosophy and science was inevitably based on the Aristotelian concept of homogeneous space and time since they are the only kinds of space and time that could be (until the twentieth century) handled by the rational intellect—the far more subjective outlook of the Chinese being quite unsuitable for sustained scientific purposes. But this very homogeneity has also its metaphysical drawbacks. We automatically confuse things when we unfold time in space; homogeneous time is only an *extension* symbol of true duration; numerical multiplicity is only an extension symbol of the qualitative multiplicity which we find in the thought-forms of duration.

The Western mind has therefore been inclined to confuse symbol with "fact," and take the shadow of the *thinking* "I" projected into homogeneous space and time for the real, *living* "I." So that it all depends on whether we look at our mental state in time-quality where it really happens, or in time-quantity, where we project it. Which one of us has failed to experience some crisis or other when a few seconds by the clock seem to last a lifetime?

The objectifying mind of the West has arbitrarily extended the physical Law of the Conservation of Energy to the domain of psychology. This erroneous extension springs from a confusion between the postulated *reversibility* of all physico-chemical phenomena (an essential requirement of scientific thought and experimentation), and the non-reversibility of psychological phenomena that take place in consciousness: duration and memory constantly add the past to the present in such a way that no psychological situation can ever exactly repeat itself. Carried away by its objectifying enthusiasm, however, Western thought forgot that physical determinism had been conceived for the benefit of scientific investigation and is an arbitrary postulate of the intellect. In so doing, it has attempted to objectify the mind itself and has therefore been compelled to adopt an "associationist" conception of the mind, based on the idea that a present mental state is "caused" by preceding states, just as the state of a given physical entity is "caused" by its preceding states. Unfortunately, this outlook does not take into account the *qualitative* differences between successive states of the mind, based on the mutual interpenetration of sense-perceptions and the ever-expanding data of memory.

Physical science can predict the future because its "time" is essentially spatial, measurable, reversible and homogeneous, and is fundamentally different from the qualitative duration perceived by human consciousness. Duration implies a radical *heterogeneity* of psychological events and the impossibility of any two of them resembling the other because they both constitute two different moments of the personal ty's *history*. For a physicist or a chemist, the same cause will always produce the same effect, even when, at the microcosmic limit, science is reduced to statistical laws. For a psychologist, however, a profound internal cause will produce its effect once, and never again. Consciousness is the domain of the *unrepeatable*.

When Greek philosophy discovered the principle of causality, it was compelled by its objectifying bias to turn its back on consciousness and duration. From this sprang a mental confusion due to the fact that we use the same terms to express the relationship between two moments of our existence and the very different relationship linking two successive phenomena in the external world. The Western mind was then compelled to objectify moments of our subjective existence, assimilate them to external events and link them, artificially, through the law of causality. But, again, external phenomena in the physical world can always repeat themselves in homogeneous space–time and become applications of a scientific law; profound psychic events, involving our total personality, present themselves to consciousness only once, and no more.

This brings us to the threshold of the much-discussed problem of freedom. What is the true nature of the "I"? On the surface, that is in the conscious mind geared to act on the external world, and under the impact of sense-perceptions, there is indeed associationism of juxtaposed terms. But in *depth*, in consciousness and in the unconscious, there is less and less juxtaposition. States of consciousness interpenetrate one another; and the deeper we go, the more the *whole* personality is involved in decision-making. This, of course, is the basis of Eastern psychology.

The endless Western controversy about freedom versus necessity (or determinism) springs from the fact that the Western mind refuses to understand what the Eastern one has grasped *experimentally* from the beginning: we are truly free only when our actions spring from our *total* personality, when there is between action and personality that undefinable relationship existing between work of art and artist. The determinist illusion springs from an arbitrary effort of abstraction, from an artificial identification of the "I" that thinks only with its rational intellect, with the one that feels and acts from the depth of his being. It changes dynamic succession (duration) into static simultaneity, projects time into space and metamorphoses a *progression* into a *thing*. An occurrence is explained mechanically, and this explanation then substitutes for the actual occurrence. Strangely enough, both Western partisans and opponents of free-will believe that choice is an *oscillation in space*, whereas it is really a *progression in time*, in which the "I" and its consciousness are in a perpetual becoming. The "I" *feels* its freedom and acts upon it, but cannot explain it rationally because it has to refract it through a spatial scientific determinism.

Freedom is not analyzable, being the relationship between the concrete "I" and the act that is being accomplished. One can analyze a thing but not a progression; one can cut up extension but not duration. The concept of freedom in Western thought has been assaulted because of its inevitable incompatibility with causality's determinism—which should have been left to deal exclusively with the physico-chemical world. But this, the Westerners failed to do because, after objectifying the external world, Western thought proceeded to objectify the thinking subject himself and clashed headlong with its inherent freedom of will.

In the East, there was no such dilemma because there was no law of causality, no aggression upon the external world of nature. Eastern man is not bound by any law applicable to objectified nature—but he is indeed temporarily bound by physical nature's extension into himself in the shape of his physiology and vital instincts. Freedom, to the Easterner, does not coincide with freedom of will, as in the West, but with freedom of consciousness (*dṛk*), that is freedom *from* all potential contents, from all objects of consciousness (*dṛśya*). Therefore the Easterner will achieve freedom by mastering physiologically and mentally the factual determinism imposed by his natural instincts: thus, freedom is not an intellectual proposition in the East, not a concept of the mind but something that is systematically *developed* and lived. Freedom is a higher state of consciousness that is reached when its links with the physiological apparatus of the body have been disconnected—that is when the subject has at last neutralized the elements of the non-subject (*etat*) that are closest to it, the physical body and the thought-forms of the mind.

Unlike its Western counterpart, as has now become clear, Eastern knowledge is not limited to intellectual gymnastics: it involves the whole psyche of the subject: to know is to *become* in this space–time world—which is equivalent to *being* beyond it. This is so true that Eastern thought makes hardly any distinction between "thinking" and "willing," both expressed in India by the same word, *cetanā*.[16] The West believes that true knowledge is purely cerebral and that the conscious mind can grasp it in full intellectual detachment without involving emotion, volition or physiological processes. The East, on the other hand, believes firmly in an ontological relationship between the capacity for knowledge and the total condition of the knower; further, that the acquisition of knowledge itself *transforms* the total condition of the knower and raises his consciousness to an entirely different level. All philosophical schools of the East can subscribe to Buddha's preaching after his great mystical illumination, to the effect that he presented to his followers the experience he went through and told them to verify it themselves: "The Doctrine is not based on hearsay, it means 'come and see'."[17] He does not pretend to liberate man but to teach him how to liberate himself.

Eastern cognition does not disdain logic or rationality; it has its uses, but must eventually be overcome. Cognition is a function of transformation, not of information; it is a state of being (*bhāva*), not information *about* it. According to the *Īśāvasya Upaniṣad*, "Into blind darkness pass they who worship ignorance; into still greater darkness they who are content with (intellectual) knowledge."[18] Western discursive cognition focuses on the object, and in the last resort, on the objectified idea substituting for the material object. Eastern cognition, refusing to acknowledge any independent object, overcomes conceptual thought and neutralizes the non-subject (*etat*) by altering the subject's level of consciousness.

The East does not set much store or put much value on

the uniqueness of the individual personality, nor on its preservation in this life and beyond—hence Eastern man's eagerness to shed the superficial coating of personality, that projection of the objectified ego, in order to retrieve the real, that is the deep Self (*ātman*) which is fundamentally transpersonal. Hence, also, the remarkable balance, poise and serenity of the Eastern sage who refuses to cling to the outworn garments of the ego. Here is no Promethean fire, as in the West, but a willingness to undergo endless metamorphosis in search of ultimate reality. In other words, it is the problem of consciousness (*dṛk*) itself that fascinates the Easterner, whereas the Westerner is interested only in the objects (*dṛśya*) of consciousness, that is in ideas and abstractions. The Easterner *knows* experimentally that consciousness exists *per se*, whereas the Westerner believes firmly that consciousness cannot exist without contents, that is without objectified thought-forms on which to focus. Eastern consciousness is, ultimately, self-sufficient and can dwell in itself in a state of perfect awareness, once the non-subjective elements have been dissolved through deep and prolonged meditation, leading to eventual control and overcoming of the mind (*manonigraha*).

The great problem of the objectifying mind is to preserve the sense of *reality* of the physical world of phenomena independently of the human observer, while being fully aware of the unreliability of sense-perception when it comes to discerning the true nature of the phenomenon. The analytical nature of logical thought destroys the integrity of the phenomenon by dissecting it and cutting it down to its basic components. What saves the reality of the phenomenal world, therefore, is not analytical reason but the *logos*, *creative* reason—that is, intuition geared to the rational faculty. The *logos* prevents Western thought from looking upon the phenomenal world as mere illusion—it has its degrees of reality and its existence is saved by this *logos* which creates the intellectual concept. As *percept* loses its objective reality, in fact as sense-perception distorts all knowledge of the objectively real, the mental *concept* retrieves it by moving back and forth between concrete phenomena and the mind that grasps them. In this sense, it moves backward and forward between object and subject, linking both, yet determined to keep them apart and sharply distinct from one another. This is made possible by the fact, already alluded to, that there is a profound harmony between the intellectual processes of the rational mind and the inner structure of the physico-chemical world. The East has very well understood this and wants none of it; the philosophy of Vedānta points out that the illusionary world of phenomena (*māyā*) is the result of mental objectification (*cittadṛśyam*). And, in the same vein, the Vedāntist believes that the impersonal Brahman, when associated with illusionary *māyā*, becomes an objectified, "personal" God (*Parameśvara*).[19]

Objectified reality is thus reduced to theoretical knowledge based on the interaction between observer and phenomenon observed. But the observer himself, the subject, must then be analyzed and objectivized; his participation in the phenomenal interaction must be neutralized in an effort to understand the objective reality of the phenomenon. In classical physics, the objectified subject would then disappear as subject—by which time, the process would lose its objectivity because there would no longer be any subject to oppose it—a Pyrrhic victory. However, in contemporary physics the process of cognition ultimately disturbs the object of knowledge; therefore there will *always* be a distinction between observer and phenomenon observed, implying that the object will never be completely known— there will never be an ultimate object that can be known intellectually. In both cases, the conclusion becomes obvious: the final goal of the Western objectifying mind is simply unreachable; the identification of thinker and thought is objectively impossible. The mind cannot become its own object in spite of all the metaphysical assumptions of the West.

The situation is quite different in the East, where the subject lives in close communion with the unconscious which makes it easier to reach its final goal: the actual realization of the pure subject, that is pure consciousness devoid of contents. The Westerner objectivizes conceptually even the subject, when he can; the Easterner ceaselessly strives to dissolve all physical phenomena and mental concepts that stand between waking-consciousness and the deep Self—until he reaches mystical illumination.

Closeness to the unconscious entails a closeness to nature and to all natural processes that is unknown to the West. The Easterner is always close to nature, whatever his feelings about it—repulsion yet attraction for the motherly womb in the exuberant tropics in India and Southeast Asia, for the luxuriant vegetation that represents the unquenchable thirst for life and existence, and therefore the endless rounds of births and rebirths; delicate affection in the more temperate climes of China and Japan where man marries mother nature in such a way that it enhances nature's own soul as seen and felt through human consciousness, an aesthetic experience that is never affected, as in the West, by intellectual considerations. The Eastern work of art does not impose itself ready-made by the artist, as in the West, but draws the onlooker into itself, absorbs him but allows him to contribute and complete with his deepest feelings and insight whatever the artist left to his imagination—thus raising the onlooker's own level of consciousness to a much higher plane. Through voluntary omission, the artist penetrates deeply into the world of nature and beyond, into the essence of things, leaving behind him the phenomenal world, grasping intuitively the spirit behind the phenomenon now viewed simply as a symbol of a more profound reality concealed behind it. Quite evidently, the Eastern artist uses the same technique of concentration and contemplation that is used by the *yogī* and reaches the innermost core of the Self via a phenomenal world soon transcended. But the onlooker himself is not conceived as an entirely separate individual object, as in the West, but as another element of the subject, which eventually merges with the artist in spirit.

Western man's attitude toward nature is diametrically different—neither love nor hate but, as compared with the East, emotional detachment. Western man is the son who feels little warmth toward his natural mother; at times, he can even become hostile, as he did during the European Middle Ages; but he always views the world of nature as a wholly separate and soulless object, to be conquered and overpowered for his benefit. The modern technological mastery of the physical world is the natural child of medieval theology—just as photography is the technical child of post-Raphaelite three-dimensional painting, unknown throughout the world until then. Such revolutionary painting stunned the Easterners when they saw it for the first time, and a significant encounter occurred in seventeenth-century China when the Jesuits introduced it for the first time. One Jesuit commented on the Chinese reaction to Western architecture and mentioned that,

> ... their eyes, accustomed to their own architecture do not favour our way of building ... these large houses, those tall pavilions frighten them. They view our streets as being deep tracks carved through ugly mountains and our houses as rocks pierced with holes ... Our floors, especially, piled on top of one another, are insufferable.

And the Chinese themselves then commented upon three-dimensional painting, which gave such a realistic rendering of Western architecture, as follows: "... the Westerners take advantage of theoretical rules in their pictures which gives them a vivid representation of depth and distance. They always add shadows to human beings, houses or objects painted on the canvas . . . shadows which end in a triangular point. Their frescoes depicting buildings are so real that one is tempted to walk right in." But he adds that "such works cannot be termed real painting."[20] Of course, in the East, nature is not soulless at all but rather a womblike, motherly environment teeming with a universal life of which man partakes. Eastern man lives nature, does not think about it and does even less want to master it. There is no basic difference between animate and inanimate, organic or inorganic, between a rock or a waterfall and an animal or human being; life and consciousness are everywhere, permeate everything. As Śrī Rāmakrishna said, "When a man has true (transcendental) knowledge, he feels everything is filled with consciousness."[21]

The object–subject dichotomy in the West leads to the opposite viewpoint, since it cannot be bridged without destroying the objectifying process itself. Ever in need of violent tension between antinomies, the West pits mind against matter, soul against body. The objectified soul, for instance, is assumed to be an entirely spiritual entity which is in no way connected with the characteristics of a particular body or the vagaries of its physiological processes. It is in the body as an animal in his cage, imprisoned, with no more organic connection with it than an animal with his cage. The commentator on St. John of the Cross's *Ascent of Mount Carmel* contends: "For the soul, owing to original sin, is truly like a prisoner in this mortal body . . . and the soul calls it a 'blessed lot' to have escaped . . . from the fetters of its prison."[22] And in the scientific age, the urge to draw the whole subject along with the body into the purely physico-chemical realm became psychologically so great that it was impossible to resist; inevitably, the objectification of the subject leads to the denial of any such entity as spirit or soul. Man, thus, became a purely material mechanism, presumed to be entirely amenable to scientific analysis.

In the East, the situation is entirely reversed: the body and the mind that goes with it are presumed to be simply the closest extension of the phenomenal world of *māyā* into the subject, a cluster of instincts and desires that draw a veil concealing the deep Self. Far from being an object among other objects, the body–mind complex represents the irruption of the world of nature, overflowing with an instinctive will to existence, into the domain of the sovereign subject. The body, for instance, is not the alien prison of an objectified soul but the physico-chemical wrapping tightly knit around the Self and organically connected with it in every respect—it is essentially the "not-Self" (*etat*) of the *Upaniṣads*. The East claims that this connection has to be severed before the Self can realize itself; and this disconnection is carried out, as we shall see, by the most complex and elaborate series of psychosomatic techniques ever devised by man.

So it is that just as the philosophic contradictions such as freedom versus determinism, for instance, cannot be resolved logically in the Western context, but can in fact be overcome experimentally, so can this quest for ultimate knowledge, and therefore realization, of the Self of the Easterner be successful by overcoming the rational mind, thus disconnecting the subject from the phenomenal world of time and space. In actual fact, this squares the circle that can never be squared by strictly intellectual means. This quest, ultimately, is that of the Western mystic and the Eastern *yogī*, of the mystic as an artist of the soul and of the *yogī* as a scientist and technician of the spirit.

5 MYSTICISM AS ART

The very beginnings of artistic feeling and expression are clearly rooted in magic and religion which, in turn, are the outer expressions of some primordial mystical impulse. Even when stripped of formal religious symbolism and meaning, even when technically objectified, as most Western art has been since the Renaissance, art is still primarily intended to trigger feelings and emotions. Art does not merely copy or reproduce nature (including human nature) but reaches super-intuitively beyond the outward appearances to the core of its spirit; and in so doing, sets up a symbolic language of which the various facets of nature provide the symbolic grammar. The most important feature of artistic feeling and expression is, therefore, this "beyond"—beyond the world of the senses, yet depicted and conveyed poetically via the senses which, in turn, promote feelings and emotions. In a way, art can even become a substitute for conventional religion because it plumbs the depths that lie beyond the appearance of the physical world and provides an outlet for a rudimentary mystical impulse which is transferred from artist to audience or spectator.

Art-style is a reflection of a given culture at a given time in its evolution. The technical objectification of Western art, for instance, has come to a fateful end in the twentieth century. Just as religion has been compelled to abandon the external objective world of matter to science, so has art been forced to abandon it to technology. In fact, Western art has moved as many light-years away from its stylistic expression of the recent past as has modern physics. The first "abstractionist," the Russian painter Kasimir Male-vich declared before World War I that "In my desperate struggle to liberate art from the ballast of the world of objects, I took refuge in the form of the square." The impact of the revolution in physics on the world of art is dramatic and the evaporation of Victorian faith in the exist-ence of stable material substances prompted Kandinsky to state that "In my mind, the collapse of the atom was the collapse of the whole world: suddenly the stoutest walls fell. Everything turned unstable, unsecure . . ." He em-phasized that the importance of art does not lie ". . . on the surface, in externals, but in the root of all roots, in the mys-tical content of art . . . The artist's eye should always be turned upon his inner life . . . This is the only way of giving expression to what the mystic vision commands." Paul Klee claimed that the artist must seek to dwell ". . . in the primal ground of creation, where the secret key to all things lies hidden." And he added, "My hand is entirely the in-strument of a more distant sphere." [1]

What differentiates art from other cerebral activities which rely on discursive thinking is that it affects im-mediately and powerfully its audience, regardless of this audience's state of intellectual development—as Tolstoy pointed out in this connection, one has to first know geo-metry before one can learn and understand trigonometry; but one does not have to know how to play musical instru-ments or read musical scores to be moved by a symphony. [2] Art deals essentially with "aesthetics," from the Greek *ais-thesis*, that is the immediate, sensible contact with nature, as distinct from a logical, intellectual relationship. To an extent, the Western artist has been able to bridge the object–subject dichotomy, restoring a certain psychic bal-ance to a culture otherwise wholly dedicated to objectifica-tion. In the world of art, unlike the world of science, feeling and comprehending are one and the same. Furthermore, art can trigger a form of intuitive understanding based on feelings and emotions which are inaccessible in the shape of an intellectual argument, an understanding that is direct and participatory, very much like that of the world of magic. As Michelangelo put it, "Fine painting is by itself spiritual because the soul ascends through the effort required in order to reach perfection, that is, God; fine painting is a reflection of that divine perfection, the shadow of God's brush."[3]

Whereas science establishes an intellectual relationship between fact and fact, art establishes a relationship between fact and man, sees the symbol hidden behind the fact and, by stirring emotions, *transforms* man as well as informs him. Auguste Rodin defined art as contemplation, as the joy of an emotional comprehension of the universe and the ability to recreate it by illuminating it with consciousness.[4] So that art is really the means to penetrate the essence of appearances and convey general truths via the particular and the unique: science deals in generalities, art in the unique. But in the artist, there is also the awakening of a mystical feeling of infinite life and consciousness permeating the universe of forms and sounds; this "nature–mysticism" is the first approach, for the artist, to the full-fledged mystical rapture which occurs when the increasingly thin veil of the cosmos is torn asunder by the blinding light of ultimate reality—in which case, the mystic absorbs the artist.

Art is the depiction of inner psychological truth as seen through features in a face, tensed muscles, a melody, a rainbow or a sunset: it is essentially the conveying of such truth by means of unique emotional participation. Unlike science, it is always, in its creation as well as its impact, all at once personal and transpersonal. Both the artist and the mystic see the river of life and consciousness, *sub specie aeternitatis*, as permeating as well as underlying the visible universe; both attempt to translate this vision for the benefit of less endowed audiences. Visions, voices and stigmata are to the mystic what painting, sculpture, poems or musical compositions are to the artist—symbolic but tangible translations of their apprehension of transcendental reality into the world of common appearances. But while the artist exhausts his vision in shaping inert matter, the mystic realizes his by working on his own living person and transforming his own personality: he becomes his own work of art. In both, however, thought, love and will are fused in a unitary "power of knowing" of the whole personality: the Good, the Beautiful and the True become one experience.

On all those grounds, Western mysticism presents itself as an art rather than a science.

No two works of art are identical; and no two mystical experiences are exactly alike, whatever general conclusions can be drawn from them. It is therefore natural that, in the West, such a spontaneous gift as the mystical impulse should have been treated almost as a form of artistic activity of the gifted few—rather than, as in the East, as a quality inherent, in various degrees, in all human beings, to be deliberately developed by proper techniques. What is known to Christians, for instance, as the Beatific Vision or direct experience of God, is deemed to be unattainable by the sole exertions of the devotee regardless of his moral qualities or technical proficiency in concentration and meditation, but only and exclusively through the mediation of God-given Grace.

The great mystic Ruysbroeck, the "Ecstatic Teacher," put it this way: "Contemplation places us in a purity and radiance which is far above our understanding . . . and none can attain to it by knowledge, by subtlety, or by an exercise whatsoever; but he whom God chooses to unite to Himself, and to illuminate by Himself, he and no other can contemplate God." In Islam, Abū Yazīd of Bisṭām declared that "I sought for God for thirty years. I thought it was I who desired Him, but no, it was He who desired me."⁵ St. Augustine was utterly convinced that ". . . he had been converted and saved in spite of himself by a divine love that overwhelmed all opposition and forced him to surrender," which "led him to assert that God's grace was irresistible and that the human will was simply passive in the working out of its salvation."⁶

For Clement of Alexandria, the mystical mysteries of Christianity represent a *gnosis*, an intuitive form of cognition that is available only to the "few," not to the masses of believers; the same is true in Islam where the mystic, known to the Ṣūfīs as *'ārif*, is the gnostic or adept to whom Allah grants the Grace-like *ma'rifa*, a form of mystical understanding which pours down on him unsolicited.⁷ The mere idea that mysticism could be a science rather than an art, that mystical insight can be deliberately induced by highly technical means, repels the Western mind because it destroys the sacred discontinuity between matter and spirit on which the objectifying mind thrives—and yet, many instances of mystical ecstasies triggered by physicomental means have occurred in the West. Jacob Boehme, for instance, gazing "fixedly upon a burnished pewter dish which reflected the sunshine with great brilliance," falling into a rapture of such intensity that "it seemed to him as if he could look into the principles and deepest foundations of things"; or Ignatius Loyola, sitting on the bank of a river and facing the deep stream, whose "eyes of the mind 'were' opened, not so as to see any kind of vision, but so as to understand and comprehend spiritual things . . . and this with such clearness that for him all these things were made new." Even a lay philosopher such as Immanuel Kant "found that he could better engage in philosophical thought while *gazing steadily* at a neighbouring church steeple."⁸

The typical Christian mystical experience expresses itself in the language of ardent aspiration flowing up from human creature to God the Creator, which explains the mystic's presumed ability, in ecstasy and beyond death, to be "oned" with the Creator. This feeling is, of course, anticipatory and is closely connected with the psychological sense of linear time, linking yesterday and tomorrow with an intense longing for the future. But the Western emphasis is always put on the "distinction" being permanently maintained between the human soul and God Almighty, since the feeling of love flowing between them cannot be experienced if the individual soul is annihilated and melted away in God. And so, if theological orthodoxy be respected and a separation maintained, the mystic is compelled to describe his experience as the contemplation of two or three facets of the Godhead: the immanent Holy Spirit within and the objectified transcendent God the Father outside.

During rapture, the mystic experiences them as One; but in his description, he is compelled to adopt a dualistic position, or else adopt the Eastern interpretation and dismiss the objectified transcendent God outside as ultimately unreal; this, he is forbidden to do by the objectifying nature of the Western mind as expressed in its theologies. This dilemma plagued even Muslim mystics such as al-Ghazālī and Abū'l Qāsim al-Junayd who claimed that only Allāh exists and that man's soul is eventually "annihilated," implying a denial of one's own ultimate existence; but it was the only way the Ṣūfīs could justify the mystical experience within the Koranic constraints since they dare not speak of "union" with Allāh which would imply *shirk*, that is identification with God. When pressed because of the unsatisfactory nature of his account of the mystical experience, Ghazālī finally stated that "Beyond these truths there are further mysteries the penetration of which is not permissible"—implying that he probably sympathized with the views of al-Ḥallāj on *ḥulūl* (descent of God into the human soul) and *ittiḥād* (identity between God and the soul), but had no intention of being martyred as al-Ḥallāj was.[9] It was also, as we have already seen, the same dilemma faced by such Christian mystics as Meister Eckhart who occasionally preached absolute identity between soul and God and was condemned for it by Pope John XXII—although Nicolas of Cusa and Angelus Silesius preached in almost the same vein and escaped the wrath of the ecclesiastical authorities for no apparent reason.

As a profound student of mysticism put it in an analysis of Theresa of Avila's experiences, she ". . . set up externally to herself the definite God of the Bible, at the same time she set up within her soul the confused God of the Pseudo-Areopagite: the one of Neoplatonism. The first is the guarantee of the orthodoxy of the second, and prevents her from losing herself in an indistinction which is non-Christian. The confused God within is highly dangerous . . ."[10] The doctrine of the Trinity made it relatively easy for the Christians to perform this artifice; but it was more difficult for such rigid monotheisms as the Jewish and the Islamic to rationalize; even the Kabalists and the Ṣūfīs were compelled to express themselves within the confines of their respective orthodoxies, for fear of sharing the dismal fate of al-Ḥallāj.

Western mysticism is a form of art because, unlike its Eastern counterpart, it is essentially based on that most admirable of all emotions, *love*—that is, on an ardent desire to reach imperishable, absolute Beauty and Goodness. Whereas Eastern mysticism is mostly based on a form of translogical cognition, the Western mystic strives to reach a *vision* of the Godhead through sheer love while preserving the full autonomy and reality of his personality. This concentration on love entails, in turn, a certain feminine passivity on the part of the Western mystic since he waits for and expects to be captured and ravished by God's Grace.

This passivity implies letting oneself go and becoming wholly receptive. The painter Raphael once told Leonardo da Vinci: "I have noticed that when one paints one should think of nothing: everything then comes better." And very much like the great artist, the mystics open themselves to whatever emotions well up from their inner depth. Theresa of Avila advises: "Let the will quietly and wisely understand that it is not by dint of labour on our part that we can converse to any good purpose with God." Or Meister Eckhart: "The best and noblest way in which thou mayst come into this (mystic) Life is by keeping silence and letting God work and speak. Where all the powers are withdrawn from their work and images ... the more thou canst draw in all thy powers and forget the creature, the nearer are thou to this, and the more receptive." Another expression of this attentive passivity is given us by Boehme:

> When both thy intellect and will are quiet and passive to the expressions of the eternal Word and Spirit, and when thy soul is winged above that which is temporal, the outward senses and the imagination being locked up by holy abstraction, *then* the eternal Hearing, Seeing, and Speaking will be revealed in thee. Blessed art thou therefore if thou canst stand still from self-thinking and self-willing, and canst stop the wheel of thy imagination and senses.[11]

The mystical trance comes upon the Western devotee unexpectedly, can occur with lightning speed anywhere, at any time; it is not the mystic who tries to come closer to God through technical proficiency but the Almighty who overpowers and captures him in the brutality of the ecstasy; and operating through the free gift of Grace, it is the Almighty who decides when and how the mystical rapture is to take place. Some fortunate Western mystics undergo their first experiences when they are ten or eleven years of age; others go through a lifetime of penance and asceticism without undergoing any profound experience—all are at the unpredictable mercy of God's Will. In other words, in the West there is no sophisticated method, no scientific technique whereby one becomes a mystic; one has to be born such as one has to be born an artist.

The difference between artist and mystic springs from the fact, already alluded to, that the artist communicates his insight, and sometimes ecstasy, by shaping forms, sounds or colours; he attempts to translate the truth of the "Beyond" into the beauty or ugliness of *this* time–space world. But because his insight is not as profound as that of the great mystic, it is often more successful in communicating his emotions, and through his emotions, the metaphysical meaning and ultimate reality hidden behind the phenomenal world. In a sense, art can be considered the succedaneous achievement of someone who can *do* but cannot simply *be*. It is, however, far more difficult for the mystic to describe, even in the most poetical language, his far more profound experiences which are truly "ineffable" and cannot possibly reach his audience in such a way as to have it share his subjective experience; only the artist, as a true nature-mystic of a lower order, can do it. As expressed by a historian of Western mysticism,

> Mysticism, the most romantic of adventures, from one point of view the art of arts, their source and also their end, finds naturally enough its closest correspondences in the most purely artistic and most deeply significant of all forms of expression.[12]

There is one noteworthy exception to the fact that, by and large, Western mysticism is a form of art rather than of science: Ignatius Loyola's *Spiritual Exercises*. Here, for the first time in the West, mysticism is treated almost as science and technique rather than art. For the first time, it is handled in almost Yoga fashion, brought under the control of the human will, disciplined. Every impulse of the exercitant is made to conform to a definite psychological pattern; the inner life and imagination are not left to arbitrary moods of the moment but brought under the imperious commands of volition. The *Spiritual Exercises* severely mark out the necessary stages of the mystic's progression and their required sequences, and just as sternly warn that no "foreign emotion, however noble, should interrupt the prescribed course, so that when lamentations over sin or the pains of death should be tasted, the consolation of redemption and resurrection should not intrude, out of its place." [13]

The *Spiritual Exercises*, without the benefit of the considerable knowledge of psychology and physiology of the greatest Indian *yogīs*, go so far as to prescribe what the outward bearing of the exercitant should be during meditation, how to breathe in and out, what his bodily posture should be. In order to vitalize desired concepts, it prescribes the specific time when the cell should be darkened, when the exercitant should look upon a skull or when he should contemplate fresh flowers in order to call to mind "the blossoming of the spiritual life." All such exercises to be performed under the direction of a "Master of the Exercises," a sort of Jesuit *guru* who adapts the schedule to the particular aptitudes of the exercitant.

This unique introduction in the West of a proto-scientific harnessing of the mystical phenomenon, along with its *perinde ac cadaver* discipline and spiritual militarization, goes a long way to explain the extraordinary performances of the Jesuits in history.

We know that the main problem of the Western mystic is that, unlike the Eastern one, he has to *relate* to a Godhead that is and always will be presumed to be utterly distinct from himself. Many times, this relationship breaks down and almost all mystics have gone through this phase of atrocious feeling of being abandoned and desperately alone. [14] The great Western fear is that of falling into utter subjectivism, either letting the "Holy Spirit" take over completely and clash with the dogmatic theologians of the Church, or, alternatively, letting the Devil take over and impose its Satanic forms of insanity on the soul: Luther faced this psychological problem when he threw his ink-pot at Lucifer's phantasm. The Western problem is, therefore, to keep control of the mystical impulse and channel it in what is considered to be the right direction—Biblical, Evangelical or Koranic, as the case may be.

Many natural mystics, born with the holy gift, are tempted to bypass the stage of meditation in order to reach contemplation right away. But, in the Western context, the obligation to meditate before letting oneself go straight into contemplation is imposed by the ecclesiastical authorities to ensure that the mystical impulse is kept under control—that is, steered in the "orthodox" direction. In fact, meditation slows down the mystical process and often hampers it, to the great inconvenience of the mystic. Theresa of Avila complied under duress at the request of her "director of conscience" and stated many times that orison and meditation impeded the mystical experience. The fact that she reached the stage of pure mystical rapture only in her early fifties is entirely due to Loyola's insistence that she develop her senses, memory and imagination—all things for which she felt that she was not gifted, as she herself stated—and focus them on specific objects: the concrete suffering of the damned, the happiness of the elect or various attributes of the Almighty.[15] But John of the Cross, while accepting the fact that meditation was necessary in the early stages of mystical development, stated clearly that concentration on such themes as Jesus on the Cross or God the Father seated in full majesty on His celestial throne (*objects* of consciousness) was *not* conducive to the "divine union," that is, to mystical ecstasy.[16]

Obstacles and difficulties all proceed from the fact that there is a fundamental opposition between the Western forms of meditation and spiritual contemplation. Western meditation is essentially rational and analytical, and unlike Eastern forms of meditation, aims at intellectual clarity; contemplation is synthetic and intuitive, and rejects or rather overcomes words, concepts and images, that is all things that are relative, limited, finite. In fact, in the Western context, it is quite clear that everything is done to obstruct the normal development of the mystical impulse; and rare are those Westerners who adopted the reverse Oriental technique of overcoming the process of intellection altogether.

The result of this cultural obstruction, which is directly traceable to the objectifying process of Western consciousness, is that the Western forms of meditation mould the mystic in such a way that he is eventually compelled, under theological compulsion and the anthropomorphic bent of the West, to strive for contemplation of a *personal* God. Thanks to meditation, Western style, the ecclesiastical authorities insert their *objective* theological legislation into the purely personal and *subjective* experience of the mystic and shape it to suit their orthodoxy: this grafted tree is not the natural tree, as it is in the East where the graft is thrown away when no longer needed. For all this insertion of clerical authority in the natural process of mystical development, it still remains that the Western outlook emphasizes the pre-eminence of the "supernatural," miraculous gift from God, the spontaneous descent of Grace into the soul which no amount of meditation, alone, can conjure—but can easily obstruct. John of the Cross emphasizes that even after the "night of the senses," followed by the "night of the spirit," man still remains powerless; his will cannot break through the ultimate barrier; only God can then send his Grace that will overcome all obstacles and lift the mystic up to the contemplation of Him. All previous exertions willed by the mystic are merely preparatory and can only take him to the threshold. There is therefore complete discontinuity between man's mystical efforts and the ultimate contemplation of the Almighty; and the name of that discontinuity is God's Grace.

For all the meditational disciplines devised by the Western creeds to keep full control of the "dangerous" mystical impulse, there is basically no scientific understanding of the psychosomatic phenomenon itself comparable to the growing scientific understanding of purely physical phenomena. Western mysticism remains an art and the Western mystic remains an artist; not least in that art that he practises are the innumerable devices and artifices whereby he manages to slip by the orthodoxy of the official theologies and convey in his messages and descriptions the subjective states of being that often come close to the Eastern experiences. Tauler's following words, for instance, might just as well have been written by an Easterner:

> His spirit is, as it were, sunk and lost in the Abyss of Deity, and loses the consciousness of all creature-distinctions. All things are gathered together in one with the divine sweetness, and the man's being is so penetrated with the divine substance that he loses himself therein, as a drop of water is lost in a cask of strong wine. And thus the man's spirit is so sunk in God in divine union, that he loses all sense of distinction.[17]

Meister Eckhart went even further when he stated that "If I am to know God directly, I must become completely He and He I: so that this He and this I become and are one I."[18] This is, of course, pure monism.

The lack of scientific understanding of the mystical phenomenon is largely responsible for what John of the Cross has called the Dark Night of the Soul—a terrible Sahara of the spirit during which the parched soul loses all vision of God, feels abandoned and utterly alone in sheer spiritual darkness, suffering the agonies of the damned. It is significant that Catherine of Genoa, describing this journey through the Dark Night and explaining it by the fact that God cannot enter a soul that is still sinful, tells us of her tears and of an internal fire of such intensity that it would have "calcinated a diamond."[19] This particular phenomenon is explained clinically in the East, as we shall see,* by the fact that the psycho-physiological apparatus, and especially the nervous system of the devotee, is too weak and unprepared for the unexpected violence of mystical ecstasy; and that a complete physiological renewal of the physical body must take place before this Dark Night comes to an end.

For the Western mystic, constantly supervised by often uncomprehending spiritual "advisers" and confessors, there can be nothing but self-contempt during this atrocious phase; and, as Theresa of Avila put it, "You would be terrified if God showed you how he treats mystics ... The tribulations he inflicts on them are intolerable. Those who lead a normal active life ... imagine that in this state everything is light and sweetness. And I state that it is highly likely that they could not stand for a day sufferings that are current among contemplatives."[20]

Theresa of Avila formulates clearly the Western outlook when she claims that the mystic seeks two items of knowledge: knowledge of the "I" and knowledge of God—both being fused in One in the Eastern monistic conception. When God is hidden during the Dark Night, it is precisely the time when the real nature of the sinful "I" discloses itself, with all its weaknesses and vices entailing a state of utter despair and an irresistible urge to plunge into hell out of "hatred of God."[21] All recollections of the first stages of bliss are either forgotten, or explained away as being delusions due to feverish imagination or the Devil's work; the idea that one is damned for all eternity becomes overwhelming. Meditation and concentration become increasingly difficult, the soul becomes anaemic and the unfortunate mystic is overpowered by an immense feeling of lassitude: this is the stage known to Western theologians as "spiritual aridity."[22] The desperate feeling of being abandoned by God leads to immense sadness, anger, then weakness and fatigue leading to a longing for death: all this of

*See p.140

such overwhelming nature that it has been termed "negative ecstasy." [23]

Those mystics who survive the Dark Night of the Soul
claim that this crossing of the spiritual desert with all the
suffering that it entails is necessary as a preparation for the
final stage: the permanent contemplation of God. During
this crossing, all the vices and evil features of the "I" die
away, leaving it pure and totally humbled and unselfish;
whatever elements of pride, vanity and egotism had been
triggered by the first ecstasies are burnt away, making room
for a feeling of complete humility; and the desire for a permanent contemplation of the Divine eventually overwhelms
the mystic. Such is the purpose of the Dark Night of the
Soul of Western mysticism.

On one point, both Eastern and Western mystics agree:
ecstasy and rapture are not the final, ultimate stages in the
mystic's progression but are only temporary states on the
way to the final and permanent contemplation of the
Divine; and both agree that this *theopathic* or "unitive"
state (Indian *samādhi*, Japanese *satori*), this *mysterium in-
effabile*, is extremely rare and that most mystics remain at
some stage or other below it; only the spiritual "geniuses"
reach it. And it is in this theopathic state, where all symbols, concepts and representations are transcended that
even Western mystics can hardly resist the claim of complete fusion between soul and God. Theresa of Avila even
managed to let us know that in this state which she terms
the "Seventh Mansion," the soul unites with God in such a
way that ". . . it becomes the same thing . . . the soul appears to be more God than soul . . . the Divine Marriage
lifts the soul above itself, makes it Divine and makes it God
through participation." [24] That is about as far as a Western
orthodox mystic dare proceed.

Both in the East and in the West, the great mystic can
only translate his experiences in picture-language whose
succeeding pictures annihilate one another; in a self-tran-

scending lyricism, this language is almost entirely based on negatives, although less so in the West than in the East—as Suso put it, one must "annihilate one picture with the help of another."[25] So that between the living experience of the subject and the official theological doctrines, this picture-language constitutes an aesthetic, artistic intermediary which partakes of both, being all at once a living experience and an explanation of that experience in terms of symbols that are familiar to a particular culture and to its religious expression. Quite clearly, a Muslim mystic will not be afflicted by stigmata or visualize the Cross. And in the case of such great mystics as Ruysbroeck (also suspect of heresy in his time for his identification of the soul with God), they can even become the founders of new literary languages. It is the mystical experience itself that creates beauty; the symbolic development that springs from it is spontaneous, unpredictable and exhalting—the fount of the purest form of poetry there is.

In the Western context, there is complete identification between sin and ugliness—only a pure soul can contemplate the beauty and magnificence of the universe and of the spirit underlying it. Jalāl-ad-Dīn Rūmī advises: "Reconcile yourself (with God), cease revolting against Him so that the earth from which water springs appears to you as a carpet of gold. I, who am constantly at peace with the Father, look upon the world as Paradise; each moment, it assumes a new form and a new beauty." Far from despising or hating the world as is the fashion among ascetics at the beginning of their training, the great Western mystic undergoes an aesthetic experience when he contemplates the world and, through the world, the spirit or consciousness that underlies it; John of the Cross expresses it when he speaks of "The great joy of this awakening, of this knowledge of God through his creatures."[26] It is almost the discovery of a new form of artistic feeling and expression in the mystery of the mystical experience.

The general aim of Western mysticism is not the dissolution of the personality in the Divine as in the East, but a creative effort to generate a new, pure personality devoid of all the sins, vices and ugliness of the old one. Love, the prime emotion that propels the Western mystic toward his goal is a sublimation of profane love, a dynamic impulse, but also a disinterested one, to join Jesus' sacred heart or the Virgin Mary's sorrowful one or an impassioned longing for the Divine Lover, the Godhead: St. Jerome pointed out that "Plato located the soul in the head; Christ located it in the heart." According to Dionysius the Areopagite, "Divine love draws those whom it seizes beyond themselves: and this so greatly that they belong no longer to themselves but wholly to the Object loved."[27]

Most of the accounts of the main Western mystics read like love stories; they sound almost drunk with love. This applies to Muslim mystics as well as to Christian ones, with this slight difference, especially among the Persians, that this love has often homosexual connotations; in order to induce an ecstasy, al-Ghazālī had to contemplate a beautiful male youth.[28] One way or another, mystical love in the West clearly points to sublimated eroticism, which is inevitable inasmuch as contemplation of an objectified and separate Godhead and the striving to come closer to It can only be achieved this way, with the assistance of the lowest as well as the highest faculties in man: John of the Cross explains that "Sensuality often awakens during the course of spiritual exercises; it is not in the power (of the mystic) to prevent this and it sometimes happens when the soul applies itself to the most sublime orison."[29] Almost against their will, Western mystics will often truthfully admit the considerable participation of physiological processes during raptures; Ruysbroeck attempts to distinguish as sharply as he can human and Divine love, yet has to admit that the physical body experiences a "voluptuous feeling" during the experience of Divine love; Theresa of Avila acknowledges the fact that during ecstasy "... the body plays a considerable part."[30]

Other semi-physiological phenomena were often noted by Western mystics, although often explained away with the help of metaphors and allegories—the blinding inner light that usually accompanies mystical ecstasy, the feeling of inner fire and heat of such intensity that the mystic "... groped my breast, seeing whether this burning were of any bodily cause outwardly. But when I knew that only it was kindled of ghostly cause inwardly, and this burning was naught of fleshly love or desire, in this I conceived it was a gift of my Maker."[31] Or again, Jacob Boehme: "Now while I was wrestling and battling, being aided by God, a wonderful light arose within my soul. I recognized the true nature of God and man, and the relation existing between them, a thing which heretofore I had never understood, and for which I would never have sought."[32] And yet again, unlike their Eastern counterparts, Western mystics never attempted a systematic analysis of the correlation between physiological processes and spiritual experience.

Even so, the language of love used by most Western mystics must not mislead us—it is entirely allegorical, and uses conventional symbols that antedate the beginning of Christianity and Islam. Lacking the profound knowledge of the East and unwilling to undertake an exhaustive and methodical survey of the mystical experience's psychosomatic manifestations, Western saints had to rely on the conventional literature of the past—more especially on the Song of Songs which was interpreted as a symbolic dialogue between the Messiah and the Church. Both tradition and cultural necessity compelled Western mystics to translate their experiences into a hoary but inadequate symbolism which became something of a straitjacket for them. But even that small element of erotic feeling which slips in once in a while disappears totally when the higher reaches of the mystical experience are entered; and then, like all other

mystics all over the world, the Westerner must acknowledge that language simply cannot render an account of the
lived experience which is truly "ineffable." It is not for lack
of trying; here is one of the early Christian accounts by
Clement of Alexandria in the second century A.D.:

> These gnostic souls are carried away by the splendour of
> the Vision, and being reckoned as holy among the holy,
> and rapt away, they attain to the highest of all regions,
> and then, not in or through mirrors do they greet the
> Divine Vision, but with loving hearts, they feast eternally
> upon that never-ending sight, pure and radiantly clear,
> enjoying a delight that never cloys, unto unending
> ages.[33]

Gnosis is the outcome of contemplation and means the
Vision seen by the eye of the soul thanks to the inner
light—and has nothing to do with ordinary faith, however
pure and complete it may be. The Vision to which Clement
of Alexandria refers is a vision of Beauty in the sense Hegel
gave it: "Beauty is merely the spiritual making itself known
sensuously." It is this that makes the saga of Western mysticism into a strikingly aesthetic experience; and in the
course of the developing mystical experience, the break-
through occurs when sensuous beauty finally turns into the
Sublime; at that point, the artist of the spirit finally turns
into a full-fledged mystic.

6 MYSTICISM AS SCIENCE

The word "science" derives from the Latin *scientia*, that is "knowledge." In Greek, however, it was known as *epistēmē*, from the verb meaning "standing up to," implying confrontation between subject and object. Natural science has come to mean, in modern times, knowledge of physical phenomena based on systematic and unbiased observations; examination of the results leads to classification, from which, in turn, general rules or laws are deduced. Thereafter, these laws are applied to new observations; if they fail to correspond exactly to the new observations, they have to be altered or scrapped altogether until such time as an exact correspondence between observation and law is reached. What all this amounts to is that natural science's goal is inductive *predictability*, the ability to foresee the future thanks to scientific laws: science, fundamentally, is the search for judgements for which it can obtain universal assent. Whereas art conveys the particular expression of a general feature, science creates laws in which the general swallows up the particular.

Except in a few isolated instances, the Greek scientific effort never went beyond the stage of observation. Distrustful of the data given by sense-perceptions, the Greeks retreated into a search for the *autonomy of thought* (conscious and rational) from external constraints—rational thought being seen as a surer guide toward ultimate reality than the deceptive senses. The Greeks did establish the ground rules of logical and analytical thinking along with its mathematical apparatus, but they failed to *question* nature. It was left to the post-Renaissance West, starting with Copernicus and Galileo, to reach the stage of a continuous dialogue between man and nature by adding scientific *experimentation* to mere observation. This was the pragmatic stage whereby rational thought decided to create the circumstances in which it not only observes nature but sets the stage for the observations, initiates the physical occurrences and thereby "experiments"; thereafter, it is left to nature to answer "yes" or "no." Mere observation cannot exactly determine the respective contributions of all the factors that go into producing the phenomenon observed: this, the experiment can do by isolating the one factor it is studying from the others and apply the law of causality to it. This leads us now to redefining science: it is not so much knowledge as the "making of knowledge."

Contemporary physical science handles the outer world on its level, the level of *phenomena* which, originally, meant "things that appear," or "appearances"—which can only appear to the extremely limited senses that we possess. Progress in physical science is thus based on observations, hypotheses linking such observations, testing and experimenting, and when success is achieved, on the establishment of physical laws whose essential value is their *predictive* quality.

On all counts, by the aforementioned definition, the East has handled the mystical phenomenon "scientifically," or at the very least, proto-scientifically. This is made all the easier in that science is, by definition, totally *impersonal* and that in the East, the person or personality is not conceived as having any intrinsic and durable reality.

The fundamental difference between these two sciences is that Western science studies physical nature, whereas the Eastern one scrutinizes *human nature*—the difference between the outer and inner universes. Essentially, Eastern science studies life and consciousness from the inside, as lived and experienced by the inner being. While the pre-Socratic Greeks looked out of themselves at the visible universe and sought for an explanation of the *physis*, the nature of the physical world, the Indians, for instance, gradually turned their backs on it and began to look inward, into their psyche (from the Greek *psukhē*, meaning breath, life or soul). What began to fascinate the Easterners was the human condition, the conditioning of man and, more important still as we shall see, his "deconditioning."

But whereas Western physical science is objective, the Eastern psycho-physiological science is mostly *intersubjective*, that is mostly based on the personal relationship between like-minded *guru* and disciple within the framework of a psychosomatic technique. The fundamental difference between the two inquiries is that natural sciences and especially physics study the "existent" (from the Latin *ex-sistere*, "being outside ourselves"); whereas Eastern metaphysical science aims at reaching the transcendental "real" by proving experimentally that what exists is basically unreal.[1] This distinction was made by India's greatest mystic-philosopher, Śaṅkara, in his exposition of Vedānta philosophy. This proto-scientific approach of the East also accounts for a certain coldness in Oriental mysticism, as compared with the gushing affectivity and lyricism of the Western variety. In the East, the key word is *vairāgya*, "passionlessness," or "detachment."

Being largely indifferent to an objective world and believing in the sole reality of the deep *subject*, the East has studied the mystical "way" of internal metamorphosis *pragmatically* and non-dogmatically, with almost clinical thoroughness—whereas the West, encumbered by dogmas and Holy Scriptures, has never developed what could be called a methodical science of the "way" based on observation and experimentation. Ironically enough, there is even a strong link between mystical insight and the understanding of the physical universe. In China, for instance, it is noteworthy that it was the mystical Taoists rather than the positivist Confucianists who developed a remarkably modern understanding of the physical universe, reminiscent of that which is disclosed by Relativity. Joseph Needham tells us that the Taoists were "... at one and the same time scientific and mystical,"[2] and proceeds to point out, quoting the Ming Chia (logicians) school of philosophy, that their basic insight was that of "The Tao as the Order of Nature ... brought all things into existence and governs their every action, not so much by force as by a kind of natural curvature in space and time ..."[3]—an anticipatory vision of the universe of modern physics.

The paradoxical meeting between Eastern mystical insight and contemporary physics springs precisely from the fact that both disciplines are thoroughly *empirical* in their inquiries. Both are experimental, both observe with detachment—easily in the East since ego and personality have to be dismissed as fundamentally unreal. They are both free from intellectual bias and while they question physical nature in the West, they study human nature in the East, along with the mutations of its psycho-physiological apparatus (*abhyāsa*). Where these two sciences are bound to meet is when physics comes close to the fundamental nature of the universe, to the world-stuff which is mind-stuff, that is consciousness. This meeting would not have been possible a hundred years ago when physical science held almost dogmatically a far more deterministic and mechanistic view of the physical universe, a view that is still quite useful as far as our everyday life is concerned but which is no longer appropriate at the microcosmic level— the very edge of the material world—where problems of consciousness intrude unceasingly. The phenomena analyzed by quantum physics, for instance, are elements in a string of processes and what binds them together lies in the observer's mind. The fundamental unity of all things and events at that basic level is bound to include human consciousness. It becomes, therefore, increasingly evident that, as stated earlier, both the scientific approach in physics and the Eastern mystical approach are complementary rather than opposite and antagonistic.

From its early days, Greek philosophical thought focused on the various *theoria* of the objective order of things, first physical things and then, mental objects. From the *atomos* of Democritus to the "ideas" of Plato, we find this almost exclusive pursuit of the structure of the objectified world. Not so with the Indians who soon forsook the contemplation of the phenomenal world of nature that so fascinated the Greeks; unlike them, Indian logicians began to study empirically the structure of human *language* as paramount manifestation of the human condition. It is true that both Socrates and Aristotle discussed the content of concepts in language, the limitations imposed by the forms of language, the structure of logic and so forth. Plato and Aristotle were aware, however, only of noun and verb; Aristotle added conjunction and articles when writing about the rules of rhetoric; but their work in this respect cannot compare with the vast scope of their Indian contemporaries.

From the early exegesis of the first holy books, the *Vedas*, to the technical interpretations given by the Mīmānsā, we find the Indians analyzing their own religious and literary texts—which led inevitably to the development of a philological science, expounded in the *Vedāngas*, dealing with phonetics, grammar and etymology, with which the Greeks had nothing to compare.[4] The development of Indian culture is studded with the names of brilliant grammarians such as Pānini (*c.* 350 B.C.), who wrote the earliest scientific grammar in the world, Kātyāyana, and the celebrated Patañjali (second century B.C.).[5] The sounds corresponding to the letters of the Sanskrit alphabet were classified systematically, vowels and diphthongs separated from

semivowels, sibilants and mutes. The sounds were classified according to the various places in the mouth from
which they originated—gutturals, palatals, cerebrals, den-
tals and labials. Words were analyzed, their roots uncovered and flexibility introduced with the addition of prefixes
and suffixes.[6] Is it any wonder that the Western discovery
of Sanskrit late in the eighteenth century triggered the rise
of Western comparative philology? At any rate, the logical
analysis of the potential resources of language gave the
Indians the conviction that they were tapping the sources
of a rigorous knowledge of human nature. In other words,
the Indians had thereby decided to create a *psychological*
rather than a "physical" science; they did this as a means to
an end—the understanding of the human condition.

However, a mere "intellectual" understanding of the
human condition was not what the Easterners were after; it
was to be only the beginning of a process of inner discovery
that led them from philology to psychology and to a profound study of the unconscious, its processes, the myths
and symbols that sprang out of it and which they always
respected as being of far greater psychological value than
any scientific understanding of the physical world. But
beyond the understanding, they looked for action: the "deconditioning" of the human individual, the stilling of the
chaotic mental activity that goes on in the dream-state as
well as in the awakened state. They sought for domination
and mastery over this involuntary activity of the mind
(*antahkarana*, the "inner instrument") which stood as a
screen between the ephemeral personality and the deep
Self; and so, they began to develop a veritable science and
technique (*upāya*) aimed at achieving this mastery by "burning" all the random contents of consciousness as one
polishes a mirror in order to enable it to reflect reality.

It is largely to the Sāmkhya and Yoga schools of philosophy that the East owes its science of depth psychology,
later on adopted by Buddhism. Theirs was the first strictly

psychological interpretation of human existence—meticulous, positivist. Their psychological functionalism turned its back on Vedic sacrificial ritualism which still looked out at the external world: the only reality was to be found in the subjective states of consciousness. The end-result of psychological introspection, according to Sāṁkhya, is the liberation of the life-monad, the spirit (puruṣa) from matter (prakṛti), in other words from the clutches of both the physical body (sthūla), which disintegrates anyway at the time of death, and of the subtle body (sukṣma) which carries human personality beyond death through the cycles of reincarnation. Then the science of Yoga comes into play because it is the dissolution of the subtle body that is the basic aim of the process of disconnection: once this is achieved, the process of reincarnation comes to an end and pure unconditioned consciousness is reached.

That Eastern thought has always been hankering for practical methods and systems of mystical introspection is made clear when Buddha, the shining star of the Eastern weltanschauung, replies to the metaphysical and cosmological speculations of Hinduism that his system is not a philosophy (darśana) but a pragmatic, technical "method" (yāna) designed to bring about liberation.[7]

The theoretical foundations of this science of the psyche were laid at the time of the Upaniṣads when polytheism was outgrown, but not destroyed as in Greece. Deities are still accepted as subjective realities within the psyche; soon enough they lose whatever objective reality they were ever assumed to have had and become strictly existential—they all become iṣṭa-devatā, deities from among whom one may choose whichever is more suitable to one's temper and personality: they become fundamentally illusory. Furthermore, they were understood no longer as specific individual deities endowed with proper names but as symbolic ranks or titles, indicating a specific psychological position (sthāna-viveṣa) as emanations of the Absolute: he who happens to occupy the position and plays the part, bears the name.[8]

The Eastern tolerance and broad-minded acceptance of all forms, all human psychological dispositions, opened up metaphysical vistas which remained closed to the West. Once and for all, it became a widely accepted fact that not only the world of nature and ritual sacrifice, but also intellectual concepts and abstract ideas are nothing but signs and symbols pointing to an ultimate mystery. The world of forms (*rūpa*) and names (*nāman*) is nothing but a distorting refraction of ultimate reality, mere contingent manifestations of an underlying substratum that can be "experienced" subjectively, but not just "thought about" in the abstract. Pure devotion (*bhakti*) can reach it and so can the negation, the "not so, not so" (*neti, neti*) of the *jnāna* technique, the intellectual weapon thanks to which the ratiocinating intellect eventually transcends itself and leaves the field open for intuitive realization.[9]

The mental world of logic and rationalism, therefore, is soon transcended by the Eastern subjective experience. What the Eastern seeker wanted to grasp were not empty shells—abstract thoughts and concepts—but the ever-living timeless reality that underlies the contingent, phenomenal world. Full acceptance of life as it manifests itself in its multifarious aspects, and a simultaneous search for the supernal Absolute beyond it, are bound to overcome a merely intellectual logic that insists, because of its very nature, on remaining on one single level of consciousness. The Eastern seeker, while still remaining in the throes of intellection, attempts to rise above it, and instead of a purely *mechanical* logic that would keep him bound to the illusory world of abstract concepts, adopts the *organic*, life-like method of dialectics, with its implied self-contradictions.

But the Eastern dialectics are only a temporary means to the ultimate end of transcending intellection altogether, whereas they are presumed to present ultimate reality as intellectual truth in the objectifying West. Both in the East and in the West, dialectics attempt to convey a higher degree of truth and reality by means of a "coincidence of opposites" (*coincidentia oppositorum*), that is identification of elements that are mutually exclusive in ordinary (Aristotelian) logic. But whereas the Western mind (Hegel) believes that it can grasp ultimate reality intellectually, the Eastern mind knows that this is impossible; in the East, the coincidence of opposites has to become flesh to the spirit, so to speak; it has to be lived and experienced by means of changes of levels of consciousness—it belongs to the domain of the mystical experience.

Without realizing it, William James expressed the Eastern outlook best in the following words:

> ... our normal waking consciousness, rational consciousness as we call it, is but one type of consciousness, whilst all about it, parted from it by the filmiest of screens, there lie potential forms of consciousness entirely different ... Looking back on my own experience, they all converge towards a kind of insight to which I cannot help ascribing some metaphysical significance. The keynote of it is invariably a reconciliation. It is as if the opposites of the world, whose contradictoriness and conflict make all our difficulties and troubles, were melted into unity. Not only do they, as contrasted species, belong to one and the same genus, but *one of the species*, the nobler and better one, *is itself the genus and so soaks up and absorbs its opposite into itself.*[10]

The goal of introspection is to overcome the intellectual "opposites." Both East and West have laboured under the impact of the "pairs-of-opposites" but their handling of them was quite different.

Many words can be defined by comparing them with their opposites—in fact, many root-words come to birth as opposite twins: mind and matter, body and soul, heat and cold, gain and loss. The analytical Western mind pits these opposites in an aggressive way as drastically opposed to one another, as *antinomies*. The whole development of Western thought appears to be based on the setting up of such sharp oppositions, which is then followed by a strictly intellectual effort to reconcile these pairs-of-opposites through the medium of dialectics—that is, again, by remaining *within* the confines of discursive thought.

The Eastern subjectifying outlook has approached the problem quite differently. Here, the absence of aggressive antagonisms transforms the opposites into contrasting and complementary *polarities*, cooperating entities like the two poles of a magnet. This more serene outlook is perfectly epitomized by the Chinese *yin–yang* dialectical alternance. The more articulate Indians saw the problem in a more intellectual way; recognizing that human languages are structurally based on pairs-of-opposites (*dvandvā*), the *Mānava-Dharmaśāstra* claims that the Godhead Itself ". . . caused the creature to be affected by the pairs-of-opposites, such as pain and pleasure." The commentator Kulluka mentions many typical pairs-of-opposites such as love and hate; but *dvandvā* was viewed as a curse to be eliminated, rather than a mighty intellectual instrument, as in the West. Not surprisingly, the *Rāmāyana* states that "Beneath the pairs-of-opposites must the world suffer without ceasing."[11] In China, dialectical thinking is most in evidence in the Mo Chia (Mohists) and the Ming Chia (Logicians) schools of philosophy. A Sinologist states that,

> The thinkers of these schools attempted to lay the foundations upon which the world of the natural sciences could have been built. Perhaps the most significant thing about them is that they show an unmistakable tendency towards dialectical rather than Aristotelian logic . . . conscious of entailed contradiction and kinetic reality. In this they strongly reinforced the tendencies which were characteristic of Taoism, just as later all these indigene-

ous logical trends were to be reinforced by some of the schools of Buddhist philosophy.[12]

The purpose of Eastern forms of meditation has always been described as being to reach "the absolute cessation of trouble from the pairs-of-opposites" (*dvandvānabhighātaḥ*) or "free from opposites" (*nirdvandvā*).[13] So that the basic difference between Eastern and Western dialectical handling of the problem is that the West seeks the solution *within* the framework of abstract thought and the East *beyond* it, for the simple reason that the West regards the pairs-of-opposites as ontological and the East does not.

This Eastern outlook explains that every intellectual conflict or disagreement was a source of synthetic wealth, every logical contradiction could be overcome by dialectical treatment. Experimental psychology and mystical introspection could develop freely without having to render undue accounts to the corrosive criticism of an Aristotelian or Hegelian logic; man's rational faculty had no other task than to register and analyze the various stages of "being" and levels of consciousness through which the seeker rose to final union between *ātman* and Brahman. Lacking the stringent and confining logic of Greek thought and the steely framework of Western religious dogma, Easterners were free to ponder upon all the great spiritual and metaphysical problems in unconditional liberty. No Indian Socrates was put to death because his opinions did not meet with the approval of his compatriots, nor was there ever a Holy Inquisition. Fierce dogmatism had no place in this metaphysical framework in which every psychological disposition, every form of belief or doubt, and every temperamental make-up could find what suited its specific requirements.

The root of Eastern wisdom is the conviction that changes of planes of consciousness can reveal a more profound understanding of reality than what is disclosed by discursive thought. In order to communicate verbally this translogical knowledge, Eastern philosophies make ample use of all the symbolism, metaphors, allegories and aphorisms (*sutra*) that were progressively brought to birth in their mythologies. The fact is that all Eastern writings and treatises were intended to lead to effective *realization* rather than merely satisfy the intellect. Easterners are not so much scientific in their texts as in their methods and deeds; many things are left unsaid in these texts, which were used mainly as mnemonic aids, because the full exposition was part of an esoteric tradition that was transmitted orally from teacher to disciple. That is why the most profound philosophic insights of the East acknowledge the ephemeral validity of polytheism and the psychological value of its symbolism.

The full emotional flavour of popular worship, the wild luxuriance of popular imagination, the manifold approaches through the multitudes of deities, each representing a specific psychological disposition, to the supreme Nirguna (unqualified) Brahman or to *nirvāṇa*, the poetic and artistic insights, everything is preserved, respected and used whenever convenient by the most abstract-minded philosopher. Mythology and philosophy walk together, in friendship and cooperation, following the *Bhagavad Gītā*'s admonition: "Let him not that knoweth much awaken doubt in slower men of lesser wit."[14] The various philosophies and creeds are not mutually exclusive as in the West but often complementary; they are adapted respectively to all forms of intelligence, from the low-brow (*māndadhikāri*) and middle-brow (*madhyamādhikāri*) to the high-brow (*uttamādhikāri*). Teaching was always rigorously adapted to the calibre of the disciple's personality. For instance, Buddha preached simultaneously the reality and the unreality of the *ātman*; his eminent follower and philosopher Nāgārjuna asked rhetorically, "Now, which of these two views represents the truth?" and then proceeded to explain that Buddha preached the reality of the *ātman* to those who were in danger of falling into nihilism (*ucchedavāda*), and its unreality to those who risked adopting the opposite error, eternalism (*śāśvatravada*).[15]

Where Greek philosophy turned its back on Olympian mythology in scorn, Eastern philosophies, wiser and more humble, learned to respect their remote ancestor—for this remote ancestor, the matrix from which they sprung, was and is not dead but is quite alive in the collective unconscious. The greatness and profundity of Eastern wisdom spring from the fact that it never lost touch with the basic realities of human nature; it always asserted that empirical truth (*aparā vidyā*) can include anything, but that it is only relatively true (*samvrti*) and is only an approach to ultimate reality.

The first step into a proto-scientific understanding of the psyche was taken when Eastern experimental psychology undertook a thorough analysis of man's unconscious processes, of their metaphysical significance and of the means whereby they could be brought under control. All forms of consciousness were studied in great detail in the *Māndūkya Upanisad*, and the normal states of consciousness were boiled down to the triadic terms of dialectics: the state of waking-being, *vaisvānara*, "common to all men" (the *koinón* of Heraclitus) in which man is conscious of the external world and of his separation from it; the state of dream-sleep, *taijasa*, which is the state of subjective inner knowledge undistorted by the impact of the separate external world—both of these states springing out of a third state which is that of dreamless sleep, *susupti*, which is equated with bliss.

The state of the human being in dreamless sleep is strikingly described in the *Brhadāranyaka Upanisad*: "As a man when in the embrace of a well-loved woman knows nothing, neither outside nor inside, so does this man, when in the embrace of the intelligent Self know nothing within or without. That is his form in which his desire is fulfilled, in

which the Self is his desire and has passed beyond sorrow."
One can see that this is a positive state of bliss, and not of
annihilation. This text adds that in this state man's spirit
(*puruṣa*) feels "I am this (world), I am the Whole" and
comments that "this is the highest world."[16] The striking
feature, as noted earlier, is that Eastern thought implies
that the stages or degrees of reality are just the reverse of
what Western man would assume. Waking-being and the
phenomenal external world (contemptuously dismissed as
"common to all men") is far less real than the dream state,
which is purely subjective, and which, in turn, is far less
real than the state of dreamless sleep.[17] Another striking
description of dreamless sleep states that "The state of
deep sleep is a unified state, a mass of wisdom (*prajñāna*)
composed of bliss . . . this is . . . the inner controller, the
womb of all, the origin and end of creatures."

The passage from one state to another is a small-scale
replica of the universal cosmogony—of world-creation,
world-preservation and world-destruction by Nirguṇa
Brahman's godly emanations: Saguṇa (qualified) Brahman,
Viṣṇu and Śiva. And beyond all these states, there is still a
higher one known as *turīya* which includes all the others as
eternity includes time, that is an awareness of timeless
unity in a state of superconsciousness in which all dialectical opposites disappear into the void from which they
were conjured, the mystical but totally lucid apprehension
of the Oneness of all. This is unification of *consciousness*
brought about by the overcoming of the *discontinuities* between these three modalities.[18] In practical terms, the technique propounded by "Dream Yoga" advises the following:

The *yogī* who can recognize dreams fairly well and steadily should proceed to practise the *Transformation of
dreams*. That is to say that in the dream state, he should
try to transform his body into a bird, a tiger, a lion, a
Brahman, a king, a house . . . or anything he likes. When

this practice is stabilized, he should then transform himself into his Patron Buddha Body in various forms ...
the Dream Yoga should be regarded as supplementary to
the Illusory Body Yoga ... for in this way, the clinging-
to-time manifested in the dichotomy of Dream and
Waking states can eventually be conquered.[19]

Having analyzed and described the different states experienced by the subject, the Eastern tradition then proceeds to lay down the actual technique for achieving its
goal: the quintessence of Yoga is the complete *reversal* of
normal behaviour, that is "going against the current" (*ujāna
sādhana*).[20] Its analysis of forms of consciousness and of
sleep suggests that the road to Self-realization lies, not in
returning as often as possible to the dreamless sleep state of
suṣupti but in moving in the opposite direction, heightening
the intensity of consciousness by overcoming all thought-
processes through mental concentration (*dhāraṇā*)—an ex-
cruciatingly difficult process illustrated by the propensity
of most beginners to fall asleep.[21]

This reversal of normal behaviour, this doing the opposite
of what life requires, is based on a highly complex technique which entails cataleptic postures of the body (*āsana*),
a complete control of breathing (*prāṇāyāma*) reaching a
complete cessation of breath for long periods of time
(*recaka*) and a total fixation of attention (*ekāgratā*): the *yogī*
makes for himself a "new body" by reversing all normal
processes. Thus it is that the state of waking-being must be
made to deliberately move in the direction of pure consciousness devoid of contents, that is a state of absolute Awareness—which, unlike the state of dreamless sleep, becomes
a lasting condition for those *yogīs* who achieve it: the goal of
the pure subject without object has then been reached. As
the man who sheds the objective world when he sinks into
deep sleep, so does the man who meditates his way through
to pure consciousness dismantle all the non-subjective ele-

ments that encumber his path to the realization of the Self.

In developing a scientific approach to the study of depth psychology and mysticism, the Eastern sages were soon enough driven to take into account the "total" personality of man—including the will, the emotions, the poetic and artistic feelings—as so many elements that had to be brought under control. In other words, the total man became a veritable "laboratory" on which psychosomatic experiments were carried out in order to develop a yogic technique which would enable all seekers to reach their goal. They soon found out that knowledge of psychology also entailed a knowledge of *physiology* and, as has already been made evident, that the two were closely linked: ultimately, it is on a thorough comprehension of psychophysiological structures that this scientific technique was based.

For instance, in his autobiography, the eminent Tibetan *yogī* Milarepa gives a striking description of this technical approach to mystical development out of his own experience:

... my physical pains and my mental disturbances increased so much that I was unable to go on with my meditation. In this predicament, thinking that there could be no greater danger than the inability to continue my meditation, I opened the scroll given me by my *guru*. I found it to contain the manner of treating the present ailment ... It was mentioned in the scroll that I should use good wholesome food at this time. The perseverance with which I had meditated had prepared my nerves for an internal change in the whole nervous system, but this had been retarded by the poor quality of my food ... I now understood what was happening; and on studying the contents of the scroll, I found it contained the accessory means and exercises (both physical and mental) which I at once began to practise. Thereupon, I saw that the minuter nerves of my system were being straightened out; even the knot of the *susumnā-nāḍī* was loosening below the navel; and I experienced a state of supersensual calmness and clearness resembling the former states which I had experienced, but exceeding them in its depth and ecstatic intensity, and therein differing from them. Thus was a hitherto unknown and transcendent knowledge born in me.[22]

Can one imagine a Western mystic expressing himself in such terms? At any rate, contemporary depth psychology has rendered justice to this Eastern discovery; it accepts the stark fact that there is a profound connection between spiritual life and physiological phenomena. It was, in fact, known centuries ago but concealed as often embarrassing; the term "odour of sanctity," for example, was coined to denote the remarkable fact that the corpses of saints appeared to decay more slowly than most, and this was a widely accepted fact. But when Luther revealed that his spiritual revelations occurred in the privy in a tower of Wittemberg monastery, shocked theologians tried their best to cover up this candid admission.[23] The fact that he was often constipated made a great contribution to his frequent encounters with the presumed Devil whom he often associated with an evil sulphurous smell. It is revealing that no one sought to analyze the phenomenon of Luther's unconscious projection of his ailment on his concept of Satan and the tight connection between his unfortunate physiological state and his spiritual life. Only in the twentieth century have Westerners been able to conceive of such psychosomatic connections which have been known and clinically studied in the East for millennia.

We must recall, again, that for the Westerner, rational and analytic, there is a complete ontological discontinuity between matter and spirit, body and soul, humanity and divinity; for the Easterner, there is none at all: everything is closely connected and interrelated, and is eventually experienced as One, when the illusion of separateness has been dispelled by the proper insight. The East would gladly sub-scribe to William Blake's saying that "Man has no body distinct from his Soul; for that call'd Body is a portion of the Soul discern'd by the five Senses, the chief inlet of Soul in this age."[24] This outlook is most obviously reflected in the etymology of the word Tantra, one of the most power-ful schools of philosophy and mysticism in India, which springs from the root *tan*, "to extend," "to continue," "to stretch."[25] This is the school that advocates a thorough knowledge of the body and its physiology in order to master the mind—"How can the *yogīs* who do not know their body . . . attain perfection?" asks the *Gorakṣa Śataka*, a technical book presumably authored by the founder of Haṭha Yoga, Goraknāth.[26]

From the start, the main emphasis is put on man's effort, will-power and self-discipline in order to "yoke" or "bind" together scientifically all the elements of the personality which are normally autonomous and scattered; also to put an end to the instinctual automatism which characterizes normal day-to-day living. As Swāmī Vivekānanda put it, "All the different steps in Yoga are intended to bring us scientifically to the superconscious state of *samādhi*."[27] Śrī Aurobindo emphasized that, "Yogic methods have some-thing of the same relation to customary psychological work-ings of man as has the scientific handling of the natural force of electricity or of steam to the normal operation of steam and electricity."[28] The word "Yoga" itself—from the root *yuj*, "to hold fast"—implies "yoking" empirical and transcendental consciousness. The following text illu-strates the psychological background:

> Know thou that the Self as riding in a chariot
> The body as the chariot
> Know thou the intellect as the chariot-driver
> And the mind as the reins
> The senses, they say, are the horses

The objects of sense, what they range over.

The text then compares the enlightened man to the good driver who has "yoked" his horses and is in full control of these elements and who, eventually,

> Reaches the goal
> From which he is born no more.[29]

The goal is translogical cognition (*vidyā*). In the East, there is no notion of original sin, divine Grace, or punishment—every man is on his own. What stands between man and his Self-realization is metaphysical ignorance (*avidyā*); and the ultimate goal of this effort is the elimination of that ignorance. The most important element in this undertaking is the acquisition of a thorough knowledge of one's unconscious (*samskāra*), followed by control over it—since metaphysical ignorance is essentially a product of an unknown or repressed unconscious.

The relationship between conscious and unconscious in Eastern mystical science is both symbolized and actually regulated by the construction of a *maṇḍala*, "circle" or "centre," usually a complex design with a circular border enclosing squares and triangles; on the periphery are four cardinal doors guarded by terrifying images whose symbolic roles are all at once, defensively, to guard the conscious mind against the disintegrating influence of the unconscious, and also, offensively, to grasp, understand and bring up to the surface of the conscious mind all the nightmarish elements of the unconscious so that they may be eventually integrated and dissolved. This is one of the most important meditational techniques of the East; it is also a well-known fact to Western psychoanalysts that when the process of "individuation" is about to take place successfully, the Western patient spontaneously creates such *maṇḍalas*.[30]

The first step of the practitioner is to become thoroughly familiar with the process of fixation of the fluctuations of the mind, *ekāgratā*, "on a single point"—whether it be a physical object, the tip of the nose, the space between the eyebrows, a mental picture or an abstract idea. One of the tools most frequently used is the hypnotic repetition of *mantras*, meaningless word-sounds; the mere fact of meditating on their non-meaning gives the seeker an intuitive awareness of the physical universe's unreality—first mental step on the road to disconnection and enlightenment. To destroy the meaning of language is to destroy also all rational mental processes and, along with them, the illusory physical world of phenomena which is hitched to the conscious mind. Meditation on paradoxical statements, enigmas and riddles also aims at the same goal, since the main quality of paradox is that it breaks the spell of logic.[31] Continuous concentration eliminates distraction, unwanted thoughts, memories, physical sensations and the like. Success is achieved when the two sources of mental chaos—sense-perceptions (*indriya*) and the involuntary activities of the unconscious (*samskāra*)—are brought under control and their products, mental whirlwinds (*cittavṛtti*) are eliminated, "burnt."

The classical yogic technique of Patañjali is divided into a number of physical and mental stages and exercises known as *angas* which have to be strenuously practised before one can hope to even reach the threshold of insight: restraints (*yama*), disciplines (*niyama*), bodily postures (*āsana*), breath control (*prāṇāyāma*), elimination of the influence of external objects on sense-perceptions (*pratyāhāra*), concentration (*dhāraṇā*), meditation (*dhyāna*). In China, the same methodical technique was in use: the Neo-Confucianist movement which incorporated elements drawn from Taoism and Buddhism, advocated concentration (*chih*), contemplation (*kuan*), mystical apprehension (*chih*) and mystical absorption (*ting*).[32] The ultimate goal is, of course, the recovery of the Self, the rapture of *samādhi*.

One of the most important components of this mystical

science is *brahmacarya*, sexual abstinence, by which is
meant not merely abstaining from the act, not merely sub-
limating it as Western mystics are wont to do—and thereby
transferring the feeling of physical lust into love on the
spiritual plane, which makes it impossible to overcome the
dualism soul-God—but "burning" and destroying the
carnal instinct altogether. Here again, in the preliminary
stages of mystical training, we have another example of "reversal" of normal processes, of doing the exact opposite of
what instinct requires: the "Left Hand" Tantric *yogī* will
often engage in sexual intercourse in order to "stop" and
then reverse the flow of semen (*bindu*) back into his body:
as the holy text specifies, ". . . the semen must not be emit-
ted (*bodhicittam notsṛjet*).[33] The same technique was used
in China where the Taoist sages made the seminal essence
(*ching*) discharge into the bladder.[34]

Yogīs can often detect by physical appearances who has
been through the burning fire of mystical rapture—for instance, the great afflux of blood to the chest which often
gives it a scarlet complexion. Śri Rāmakrishna never forgot
to examine his disciples' breath capacity and the condition
of their blood circulation before letting them concentrate
and meditate.[35] Yogīs will also use any appropriate physical
means to assist the mental power of concentration. In a
famous incident, Rāmakrishna complained to his *guru*, the
Brahmin Tota Puri, that he simply could not reach the "unconditioned" state of *samādhi*; Tota Puri looked about him,
picked up a sharp piece of glass and stuck the point between Rāmakrishna's eyebrows and thundered, "concentrate your mind on that point." And, adds Rāmakrishna,
"The last barrier fell and my spirit immediately precipi-
tated itself beyond the plane of the 'conditioned,' and I lost
myself in *samādhi*."[36]

At the very base of the Eastern mystical technique lies

the proper training in breathing (*prāṇāyāma*). All concentration and meditation depends upon the proper physiological schooling in the technique of breath-control which conditions the state of consciousness itself. The Westerner, putting the emphasis on the conscious mind, focuses his psychological interest on the brain as the seat and centre coordinating all the elements of the personality—with an occasional side-glance at the heart—and on the cerebrospinal nervous system which is considered the core of the human body. The subtle switchboard that is the brain centralizes all the incoming information flowing in from the senses and issues all the outgoing commands aiming at action on the external environment.

The Easterner, on the other hand, is in much closer contact with the unconscious and its instinctive and intuitional extensions; he therefore focuses on that part of the nervous system that is in closest contact with them—the autonomic nervous network, sympathetic and parasympathetic, which are normally below the threshold of the will's control. The autonomic nervous system functions independently of the dictates of the conscious mind; the problem is how to establish control over it, and this is where breath control comes in. Being, in part, under the control of the will, breathing can also, indirectly, influence and regulate the autonomic nervous system. Control of breath, in addition, regulates the flow of thoughts through the mind according to the Tibetan saying: "Breath is the horse and thought the rider," as well as the intensity of emotions and feelings, and therefore can bind the two nervous systems together. Invisible and impalpable, breath appears to be one opening into the non-physical dimension of man, into the pure subject—hence the elaborate techniques devised to control it in the East, in China and Japan as well as in India.

For instance, the Japanese Zen masters apply a technique of breath control to the art of archery—bow and arrow being mere tools in a process of mystical development—

that has universal applications. Here is a description, which is worth quoting at length, of the results of the application of this technique by a Western disciple:

The more one concentrates on breathing, the more the external stimuli fade into the background. They sink away in a kind of muffled roar which one hears with only half an ear at first, and in the end one finds it no more disturbing than the distant roar of the sea, which, once one has grown accustomed to it, is no longer perceived ... One only knows and feels that one breathes. And to detach oneself from this feeling and knowing, no fresh decision is required, for the breathing slows down of its own accord, becomes more and more economical in the use of breath, and finally, slipping by degrees into a blurred monotone, escapes one's attention altogether ... This exquisite state of unconcerned immersion ... is liable to be disturbed from inside. As though sprung from nowhere, moods, feelings, desires, worries and even thoughts incontinently rise up ... The only successful way of rendering this disturbance inoperative is to keep on breathing quietly and unconcernedly, to enter into friendly relations with whatever appears on the scene ... and at last grow weary of looking. In this way one gradually gets into a state which resembles the melting drowsiness on the verge of sleep. To slip into it finally is the danger that has to be avoided. It is met by a peculiar leap of concentration, comparable perhaps to the jolt which a man who has stayed up all night gives himself when he knows that his life depends on all his senses being alert ... the soul is brought to the point where it vibrates of itself in itself—a serene pulsation which can be heightened into the feeling, otherwise experienced only in rare dreams, of extraordinary lightness, and the rapturous certainty of being able to summon up energies in any direction ... this state, which is at bottom purposeless and egoless, was called by the Master truly 'spiritual.'[37]

Breath control and eventually prolonged retention (*recaka*, in India, or *pi chhi*, in China) is essential to concentration in order to plumb the depths of consciousness. While the Westerner has usually insisted that the conscious mind controls the body, the Easterner claims that this is not so because he is not in direct control of his organs and instincts as he is, for instance, of his limbs. This is why, understanding the deep connection between physiology and consciousness, the Easterner sets this connection at a low, basic level that repels the more "idealistic" Westerner.

In fact, we have almost negligible direct control over our complex body which lives its own organic and autonomous life. In order to extend our minimal control, we must acquire a thorough knowledge of our physical sensations with the assistance of a convenient symbolic imagery, based on the assumed ethereal articulations of the subtle body (*sūkṣma*) and slice it into its natural components—first step on the road to inner knowledge and mastery of the autonomous parts of the body. In other words, our mental concentration must gradually slither into these bodily sensations in order to bring them out of their usual obscurity into the light of full understanding and awareness. At no time will the *yogī* allow his mind to become distracted by random thoughts; at all times will his concentration be guided by his lucid will.[38] And as this inner knowledge increases, and with knowledge comes control, the physical body seems to detach itself from the inner "I" and begins to look increasingly like an alien envelope that belongs only to the illusory world of phenomenal *māyā*: this is the beginning of the process of disconnection, of "withdrawal of the senses" (*pratyāhāra*).

As long as the body's physiological functions take place below the threshold of the conscious mind, we tend to believe that this body belongs to us or that we belong to it; it is only knowledge and control gained through rigorous concentration and meditation that detaches it from our consciousness. But whereas the Westerner, at that stage, would proceed to objectivize and analyze those physiological processes that are brought up to the level of the conscious mind, the Easterner moves in the opposite direction: having disconnected the body from his consciousness and assumed full control over its psychosomatic functions, he becomes, like the Zen archer, uninterested in it and focuses exclusively on the liberated consciousness, the subject; he strives to become a *jīvan-mukta*, one who is "released while living." He does not raise the body to the status of an independent object: having achieved control over an efficiently functioning organism, he forgets about it and can now, deep in meditation, freely experience the fourth stage of his pilgrimage, the state of *turīya*, the "cataleptic state" in which he becomes lucidly aware of consciousness without any contents—this is meditation "without an object" (*nirmitta*).[39] It is not a state of self-hypnosis nor of trance but one of *super*consciousness. Once this is achieved, if it ever is, the mystic remains more or less in perpetual contact with transcendental Reality. Śrī Rāmakrishna once said: "You see, nowadays, it is not necessary for me to meditate much. All at once I become aware of the Indivisible Brahman. Nowadays the vision of the Absolute is continuous with me."[40] At another time, he added: ". . . I cannot utter a word unless I come down at least two steps from the plane of *samādhi*. Śaṅkara's non-dualistic explanation is true, and so is the qualified non-dualistic interpretation of Rāmānuja."[41] Quite clearly, all doctrinal or philosophic disagreements disappear for one who has reached that theopatic level.

The main problem presented by this mystical science is one of utter concentration on the variegated sensations aroused by the physico-mental exercises, concentration

made infinitely more difficult by the excruciating mono-
tony generated by endless, hypnotic repetitions. Not only
must concentration bring those sensations up to the conscious mind; it must also avoid arousing interest in them, or
sometimes in the paranormal powers (*siddhi*) that are generated by the process—a temptation which very few *yogīs* can
resist. On the contrary, the latter must be viewed with cold
detachment as alien phenomena that have nothing permanent to do with the Self—precondition for severing the link
between consciousness, on the one hand, and corporeal sensations and fluctuations of the mind-stuff, on the other. In
the process, the mind must remain constantly keen and
alert, yet detached from phenomena and sensations in order
to refrain from objectifying them. The aim is to deprive
them all of intrinsic reality. In this sense, the Easterner
does not seek to alter phenomena or control them; he does
not alter nature but *human* nature, *his* human nature. Śrī
Aurobindo pointed out that "All Rāja Yoga depends on this
perception and experience: that our inner elements, com-
binations, functions, forces, can be separated or dissolved,
can be newly combined and set to novel and formerly impossible uses or can be transformed and resolved into a new
general synthesis by fixed internal processes."[42] The Easterner's problem is to alter *himself*, that is his own psychosomatic state in such a way that all physiological and
mental phenomena eventually sink back into the illusory
world of *māyā* where they belong. Gradually, consciousness
becomes the only reality while the phenomenal world becomes increasingly unreal.

The ultimate goal has been traditionally described as
Reality (*sat*) and Awareness (*cit*), which are always brack-
eted with Bliss (*ānanda*) in the celebrated and holy formula
sat-cit-ānanda, that is the full recovery of the hidden Self
which must come to know and realize itself without any
external interference. Western analytic thought cuts up the
phenomenon in order to fit its parts into a specific philo-

sophic or scientific framework, which is then objectified; the Easterner identifies the phenomenon, but then deprives it of intrinsic reality by withdrawing his consciousness from it, which consciousness then becomes unqualified and Blissfully Aware of ultimate Reality because pure of any entanglements with objects and contents.

This Eastern detachment is not what it appears to be to the objectifying mind of the West. The achievement of personal perfection and utter serenity, this identification with the Absolute—be it of a Hindu, Jain, Buddhist, Taoist or Neo-Confucianist—does not so much inform as transform the others by virtue of setting a living example and by virtue of the natural, quasi-magical radiation that a perfected human being emanates. His is not a discursive, theoretical teaching, weighted down with philosophic, theological or scientific statements, but the practical mapping of a road on which the seeker must inevitably travel, all by himself, shedding on the way all mental constructions, conceptual theories and philosophic doctrines. The presence of the perfected human being itself works on the disciple through osmosis.

Our rational intellect cannot describe what is absolutely unique, therefore finds it difficult, if not impossible to translate direct experience into abstract concept—because Eastern knowledge is essentially *experimental* rather than theoretical; therefore cannot fix it, make it permanent and intellectually transferable. Only an actual experience can understand another one, which is the basis of the connection between *guru* and disciple. Let us return, for an example, to Zen Buddhism and the art of archery. The puzzled disciple,

> ... asked the Master: "How can the shot be loosed if 'I' do not do it?"
> " 'It' shoots," he replied.
> "I have heard you say that several times before, so let

me put it another way: how can I wait self-obliviously for the shot if 'I' am no longer there?"

" 'It' waits at the highest tension."

"And who or what is this 'It'?"

"Once you have understood that, you will have no further need of me."

Sometime later, after a great deal of practising, a significant incident took place:

Then one day, after a shot, the Master made a deep bow and broke off the lesson; "just then 'It' shot!" he cried, as I stared at him bewildered. And when I at last understood what he meant I couldn't suppress a whoop of delight. "What I have said," the Master told me severely, "was not praise, only a statement that ought not to touch you."

The amazed disciple then adds: "How it happened that they loosed themselves without my doing anything, how it came about that my tightly closed right hand suddenly flew back wide open, I could not explain then and I cannot explain it today."[43]

The methodical, systematic "mapping" of the road, of the mystical "way," is not only possible but represents the triumph of the East. The experimental knowledge acquired by thousands upon thousands of *yogīs* over thousands of years is reflected in many texts which give us method and technique; if a personal contact is needed with a *guru*, it is so that the latter can adapt the technique to the particular requirements of a specific disciple. Any attempt to dispense with a teacher entails great dangers for the disciple who risks insanity or even death. We shall refer to such an instance in the last chapter.*

Let us now select a text that straddles the two main religions of the East as an example of this pragmatic, experi-

* See p. 186.

mental and non-dogmatic approach which is typical of the scientific attitude: *The Yogavacara's Manual of Indian Mysticism as Practised by Buddhists*, which expounds a special technique of meditation on the "elements"—fire, water, earth and air. The *yogī* starts *prāṇāyāma* by focusing on the various phases of breathing by "entering into" each inhalation and exhalation. Then the *yogī* thinks and puts into effect the following: "With eye-consciousness I look down the tip of my nose, with thought-consciousness fixed on the indrawal and the outbreathing, I fix my thought-form in my heart . . ." The commentary follows up:

> When he has thus fixed his thought, alert and keen-minded, two images appear, first a dim, then a clear, one. When the dim image has faded away, and when the clear image, cleansed of all impurities, has entered his whole being, then, entering the threshold of the mind, the element of heat appears. In this, the Ecstasy has the colour of the morning star, the Preamble is golden-coloured, the Access is coloured like the young sun rising in the East. Developing these three thought-forms of the element of heat, withdrawing them from the tip of the nose, he should place them in the heart and then in the navel.[44]

Each stage of this meditation is composed of three sub-stages—entrance (access), preamble and ecstasy; each stage has its own coloured light. This particular technique, as has become obvious by now, focuses on chromatic sensations and the degree of their mental actualization measures the *yogī*'s progress toward his goal. As he goes along, he removes them further and further away or fixes them in particular "physiological" locations. It is evident, from this example, that all experiences provoked by meditations must be anchored in the psychosomatic concrete.

To repeat, the basic aim of Eastern mystical science is to bring all bodily sensations and mental activities under conscious control as the first step toward disconnection. This is not achieved by fighting against or mutilating the body—the error of most ascetics, in the East as well as in the West—but by gaining full power over all its functions via a circuitous route. It must also be recalled that this technique is a direct outcome of the Eastern form of consciousness and of its assumption that the basic problem is not one of man's *relation* with the divine but of his *identification* with it. Yogic concentration does not focus on an objectified God and an objectified soul, along with the crucial drama of the soul's ascent to God; it focuses on the stripping away of the veils of illusion by disconnecting the Self from mind and body—in fact, "liberating" himself, that is dying while still alive (*jīvan-mukta*).

The first step in that direction is the adoption of a physical posture (*āsana*) that is completely natural—the impassive cross-legged position, the juxtaposition of muscular relaxation and mental tension provided by meditation, the gathering up of all the essential organs which brings them closer together than in any other posture. The cross-legged position shapes the *yogī* into a triangle, the top angle being the seat of mental concentration, the base formed by the other two angles being the seat of the accumulation of inner energy, and the whole a symbol of cosmic self-sufficiency, of complete withdrawal from the outer world. All superfluous sensations and thoughts must be disposed of, and others brought up temporarily to the conscious mind through concentration on them and on the organs that produce them. Every element of these complex techniques is devised to achieve this utterly creative concentration as a prelude to the forthcoming "deconditioning" already referred to. Under normal conditions, we are conscious of the functioning of our various organs—stomach, liver, intestines, spleen, heart, kidneys—only when in pain. It is the duty of the *yogī* to learn and apply the proper mental and physiological gymnastics required to focus on, identify, control and, finally, disconnect these organic functions and mental activities from his consciousness.

The most striking technique of Eastern mysticism is provided by the Tāntric school which flourished mainly in
Bengal and Kashmir but permeated every part of India and
Tibet, and has many points of contact with Chinese
Taoism. This technique relies on a remarkable anatomical
diagram which bears some loose resemblance to present-
day anatomical knowledge but is, in fact, presumed to out-
line the main articulations of our subtle body (*sūkṣma*).
However much identification may take place in future research between the filament-like *nāḍīs* and nerves, for instance, or between the seven *cakras*, "centres," and the
sympathetic and parasympathetic ganglia of the autonomic
nervous system, the fact remains that the practical useful-
ness of the more or less imaginary diagram has nothing to
do with its greater or lesser degree of objective truth or
scientific accuracy. This mystical technique was elaborated
on the basis of thorough experiments with the results of
concentration and meditation, and on acute observations of
the connection between physiological phenomena and the
mental stages of the *yogī*'s progress on his "way." As a psychosomatic science looking for those physiological phenomena corresponding to given levels of consciousness, it
appears to be the Eastern counterpart of Western physics
experimenting with cloud chambers in a search for *traces* of
interactions between elementary particles—in both cases,
they can reach only *inferential* knowledge based on cir-
cumstantial evidence, since these particles are just as invisible to the eye of the physicist as states of consciousness
to those who do not experience them.

At any rate, for the purposes of the *yogī*, objectively
accurate diagrams are unnecessary; all that is required is a
rough but symbolic resemblance. This diagram will help
focus his creative imagination (*ūha*) and allow him to assert
increasing control over the organic functions by localizing
them in the chart as visualized, and externalizing them one

by one until his whole body is felt to be externalized. The apparent result of this creative effort appears to be the activation of an inner metamorphosis due to some mysterious energy symbolized by the fiery serpent-like *kuṇḍalinī*. Coiled at the base of the spine, it rises through the *suṣumṇā*, the main *nāḍī* presumed to be located within the spine; for those who have experienced it, it seems to be a definite physiological phenomenon—of which an elaborate description will be given in the last chapter.*

The descriptive emphasis put on the phenomenon of internal luminosity is also notable because, if there is one feature that all forms of mystical experience have in common all over the world, it is this "inner light" (*antar jyotih*, "essence of *ātman*"):[45] this blinding inner light is attested to as early as the *Upaniṣads* in India but it is also familiar in Christianity, Islam and even in the shamanism of the eskimos. It is the light of Moses' burning bush, the same light that prostrated Paul of Tarsus on the road to Damascus and illuminated Emperor Constantine's cross in the sky. This experience, which William James called "photism" appears to be present in almost all ecstasies.

The great adventure, the crowning achievement of the Eastern mystical science is the actualization of pure consciousness. It has no true counterpart in the West where man deals only with empirical, qualified mental processes dealing with religious, philosophical and scientific symbols, all products of objectifying cultures in which the true mystical experience is viewed with either fear or distrust, or as "subjective" delusion. This crowning achievement of the East is now having a growing impact on the West, starting with its physical sciences of nature.

* See p.185

7 ORIENTALIZATION

In the early 1650s, the French philosopher Blaise Pascal had already become famous as a mathematician and scientist of genius; he had tested in Paris the theories of Galileo and Torricelli, studied the problem of the vacuum and published his celebrated *De Alea Geometriae* in which he set up the foundations of the calculus of probabilities. Suddenly, after several months of spiritual distress, but without any preliminary warning, he experienced on November 23, 1654, what he subsequently described as the "Night of Fire" that was going to change the course of his life and make him into one of the most influential and profound writers on religious themes. Pascal had just undergone an incredible experience with a mystical rapture, which he consigned on a small piece of parchment known ever since as the "Memorial of Pascal," a copy of which was permanently sown in his doublet, and which starts as follows:

In the Year of the Lord 1654, Monday November 23, From 10.30 p.m. until half past twelve, Fire.

This two-hour-long mystical experience must have been staggering, for he consigned it breathlessly in terse words and pithy sentences, obviously overwhelmed by the dazzling vision and the inexpressible joy that swept over him:

God of Abraham, God of Isaac, God of Jacob,
Not of the philosophers and the scholars.
Certainty. Certainty. Certainty. Feeling. Joy. Peace.[1]

And so it goes on, "Joy! Joy! Tears of joy!" Here we have

one of the most lucid, articulate and penetrating masters of science and mathematics of his time, so overcome by the experience that all he can do is to stammer along, swept off his feet by an unforgettable ecstasy: for the first time in the West, at the dawn of the modern age, science and mysticism were conjoined in the same genius.

But, as usual in such raptures, they eventually come to an end. After midnight, the inner fire began to die out and the desperate Pascal cried out, "God, are You leaving me?" and when the Beatific Vision faded away for good, cried again in anguish, "Oh, let me not be separated from You for eternity!" [2] He finally surrendered, "Sweetly and totally," hoping thus to remain in contact with transcendental Reality for the rest of his days on earth.

Yet, for all his mystical predispositions and his brilliant scientific intellect, Pascal remained the typical split personality of the West—hard, analytical mind on one side, violently emotional mysticism on the other, unable to reconcile these two facets, not only of his own individual personality, but of the schizophrenic culture of Western civilization. He illustrates the fact that, time and again, the mystical impulse breaks into the Western cultural context as an alien and unexplainable intrusion which is never really absorbed and integrated by its objectifying form of consciousness. There was no room for it in a culture dedicated to locate and define the "object," and whose philosophies were constantly swinging from a Democritean materialism to a Platonic idealism, squeezing out any possibility of development of the real *subject*. There were indeed plenty of objects— *Deus* with its *machina*, causes and effects, concepts, laws, individual minds and souls—but not proper subjects, as understood in the East. Pascal's endless repetition of "Certainty, Certainty," however, does illustrate the typical feeling of being in intimate contact with some form of Absolute Reality which always accompanies the mystical insight, Reality which far transcends the objective reality sought by the Western mind within the confines of the visible universe. In the following centuries, both Western mysticism and Western physical science went their own antagonistic ways, without reconciliation nor integration—until our twentieth century brought together sciences of nature and Eastern cultures.

It was a contemporary of Pascal, René Descartes, who put his stamp on the modern era of the West by transposing the medieval Christian dualism God-soul and spirit-flesh into a philosophic one by cleaving the objective world into two sharply separate entities, mind and matter. In this new interpretation, the immanent God that was actually experienced by Pascal was raised to transcendental infinity, so far above the world that He appeared almost superfluous. The main Cartesian thrust was to separate drastically the *res cogitans*, the intellect of the thinking "I," from the *res extensa*, the objective material world extended in space and time that was now going to become the sole domain of scientific investigation. There was to be no science of the "I" in the West, no science of the subjective world. From then on, there could be no doubt as to the overwhelming success of physical science in the West. Rid of any possible contamination by the subject thanks to the Cartesian partition, the mechanics of Newton's universe came into being—a universe in which there was no real place or function for either God or human souls; it became the epitome of the totally "objective" universe.

As we know, this purely objective world has been superseded by the new philosophic outlook of modern physics, and with it, the rigid dualisms: mind–matter, soul–body, God and man—ontological dualisms typical of the analytical mind of the West—have become outdated. The Western belief in radical discontinuities, referred to earlier, is no longer tenable. Physical science now tells us quite plainly that it does not describe and explain an objectively real material world separate from us but merely a physical world subjected to our questions; physical science has now become a description of the interplay between man and the material world, nothing more; there is not, and cannot be, a truly objective picture of the universe *per se*.[3]

But even Einstein suffered from the influence of this deep-rooted dualism of the West—the same Einstein who had already partly overcome it by welding time and space together in Relativity. During the course of his long resistance against what is known as the "Copenhagen interpretation" of the Quantum Theory, he exclaimed several times that he just could not believe that "God plays dice with the world,"[4] just as centuries earlier, Descartes had claimed that "God cannot deceive us."[5] But in Einstein's unconscious, God was still atavistically the ghost of the objectified transcendental Yahweh of the Bible rather than the immanent divine spirit underlying and pervading the universe which he vaguely apprehended. Both Descartes and Einstein reacted under the assumption that the physical world really exists independently of the human observer: this is what Werner Heisenberg calls "dogmatic" or "metaphysical" realism, to which he replies that the "Quantum Theory does not allow a completely objective description of nature."[6] And he adds further that "The ontology of materialism rested upon the illusion that the kind of existence, the direct 'actuality' of the world around us, can be extrapolated into the atomic range. This extrapolation is impossible, however."[7]

This is the end of the long Western quest for total objectification that contemporary physics has now reached—and its new vision of the universe, unclouded by dogmatic or ideological prejudices inherited from the Western past, begins to look more and more like the Eastern vision of metaphysical reality.

The first important item in the Orientalization of physics

is the impact of the increasing contributioon of Eastern scientists from India, China and Japan, among others. An early indication of this trend was the collaboration of Indian physicist S. N. Bose with Einstein on a concept which became known as the "Bose–Einstein Statistics." After the two World Wars, Heisenberg noted that the great scientific contribution to theoretical physics that had come from Japan may well have been due to an affinity between the traditional philosophies of the Orient and the implications of the Quantum Theory—probably due to the fact that it must have been easier for Easterners to adapt to the quantum-theoretical idea of reality because they had not ". . . gone through the naive materialistic way of thinking that still prevailed in Europe in the first decades of this century."[8]

Many Easterners agree, and some find an Eastern flavour in the vision of the new physics. For instance, Nobel prize-winning Japanese physicist Hideki Yukawa, referring to Relativity, asserts that "Here, time resolves itself into the fourth dimension, on a par with space, where harmony prevails in an eternal state of rest . . . one may sense something close to the Oriental outlook."[9] Another striking example of the outright impact of the Eastern cultural influence is the discovery of the non-conservation of parity in the case of weak interactions by two Chinese physicists, Tsung Dao Lee and Chen Ning Yang, who received the Nobel prize in 1957. Western physicists were prompt to wonder whether the cultural heritage of the Orient had made it easier for them to doubt the symmetry of natural law.[10] It is a fact that the prime yin–yang symbol of China is asymmetrical (it is not superposable on its mirror-image, whereas the Christian Cross, for instance, is indeed left–right symmetrical). This ". . . familiar asymmetry of the oriental symbol, so much part of Chinese culture, may have played a subtle, unconscious role in making it a bit easier for Lee and Yang to go against the grain of scientific orthodoxy, to propose a test which their more symmetric-minded Western colleague had thought scarcely worth the effort."[11]

Science has now become global and intercultural, drawing into its fold an increasing number of non-Westerners who find in its new vision of the universe many elements that are congenial to the traditional cultures from which they spring. As they are quick to note, one cannot always distinguish between statements made by Eastern metaphysics, based on mystical insight, and pronouncements of modern physics based on experiments, observations and mathematical calculations.

What is really happening is a shattering of the entire world-picture of the objectifying West. If science has moved light-years away from its Victorian assumptions in the past few decades, so have—or should—all our presumptions as to the ultimate validity of Western traditional formulations in philosophy and theology. It even starts with the formulations of physics in plain, non-mathematical language—they flout all the rules of our traditional logic and sound profoundly irrational because they are translogical. They come much closer to the paradoxical aphorisms of the Indian *sūtras*; many resemble the mind-bending apophthegms of Japan's Rinzai Zen Buddhism, the riddle-like *jakugos* or the puzzling *koans*, such as the one which asks the disciple to listen "to the sound of one hand clapping." It is, in fact, no more paradoxical than James Jeans' description of the universe of Relativity as the four-dimensional surface of a cosmic sphere of which the inside is made of "empty space welded onto empty time." This is a real *koan*, and as good a topic for profound meditation as "listening to the sound of one hand clapping."

In this new vision of the universe entailed by the scientific revolution, first place must be reserved for the overcoming of the "world of opposites," previously alluded to. These hostile and mutually exclusive antinomies of Western tradition have now been transformed by scientific philosophy into alternating, interdependent and complementary *poles* like the traditional *yin* and *yang* of the Chinese. This overcoming of the pairs-of-opposites occurs constantly in nuclear physics where continuity and discontinuity coexist, where particles are all at once destructible and indestructible, where energy changes into matter and vice-versa; where the statistical character of quantum phenomena makes it impossible to state flatly that a particle exists or does not exist in a given place since it is, in fact, a probability pattern in a state that is half-way between existence and non-existence.

What we have to deal with here is a scale or hierarchy of degrees of reality or what Weizsäcker calls "degrees of truth." Explaining this concept, Heisenberg points out that "For any simple statement in an alternative like 'the atom is in the left (or in the right) half of the box' a complex number is defined as a measure of its 'degree of truth.' If the number is 1, it means that the statement is true; if the number is 0, it means that it is false. But other values are possible. The absolute square of the complex number gives the probability for the statement's being true." [12] This is how we are slowly driven away from the West's traditional logic, back to the Eastern habit of using paradoxical statements in dealing with some formulations of ultimate reality—reminding us of Buddha's statement to the effect that the *ātman* both exists and does not exist. Heisenberg emphasizes that "In the experiments about atomic events we have to do with things and facts, with phenomena that are just as real as any phenomena in daily life. But the atoms or elementary particles themselves are not as real; they form a world of potentialities or possibilities rather than one of things or facts." [13]

The partial failure of ordinary language to describe with any degree of accuracy the events of the mystical experience finds its counterpart in its failure to describe scientifically those of the microcosmic world—they are as truly "ineffable" as those of the mystical world. And just as poetry or music can, up to a point, render some of the experiences of mysticism, only mathematics can, as the most abstract of all languages, describe the new universe of physics. As Heisenberg points out again, ". . . the problems of language here are really serious. We wish to speak in some way about the structure of the atoms and not only about the 'facts'—the latter being, for instance, the black spots on a photographic plate or the water droplets in a cloud chamber. But we cannot speak about the atoms in ordinary language... the physicist has to withdraw into the mathematical scheme and its unambiguous correlation with the experimental facts." [14] What we are dealing with, basically, is potentials, "objective tendencies" or "tendencies toward reality."

The parallels with the ambiguous formulations of Eastern mystical insights are striking; these insights have always been conveyed via negative or paradoxical statements, such as the traditional "not so, not so" (*neti-neti*) of the Indians. Whereas in classical physics a thing either is or is not, following Aristotelian logic (*tertium non datur*) in which there is no room for a third possibility, this is no longer the case at the subatomic level where, as Robert Oppenheimer points out, we have the following situation:

> If we ask, for instance, whether the position of the electron remains the same, we must say "no"; if we ask whether the electron's position changes with time, we must say "no"; if we ask whether the electron is at rest, we must say "no"; if we ask whether it is in motion, we must say "no." [15]

And he concludes: "The Buddha has given such answers when interrogated as to the conditions of a man's Self after his death; but they are not familiar answers for the tradition of seventeenth- and eighteenth-century science." Indeed not; nor are they familiar in Western philosophies or theologies, whereas Eastern mystical literature is studded with such negative paradoxes, in its effort to transcend intuitively the strictly logical pairs-of-opposites. Consider the following sayings of Buddha in which he attempts to destroy once and for all the last attempts of the highly intellectualized Hindus to objectify some metaphysical concepts:

There is no Self outside of its parts.

There is a path to walk on, there is walking being done, but there is no traveller. There are deeds being done, but there is no doer.

As there is no Self, there is no transmigration of Self; but there are deeds and the continued effect of deeds.

There is no entity that migrates, no Self is transferred from one place to another; but there is a voice uttered here and the echo of it comes back.[16]

The new picture of the universe disclosed by contemporary physics appears to be largely in accord with Eastern metaphysics. For instance, if we revert to some fragments quoted earlier, we note that Relativity teaches us that space is not a fixed framework independent of its contents, but that it is part of a space–time continuum which is determined by its contents; furthermore, that gravitation is not an external "force" but is part of the celestial bodies' inherent inertia, endowed with this ability to bend light, and therefore to curve the space–time continuum. As already pointed out, the Ming Chia (logicians) school of Chinese philosophy claimed, many centuries before, that the "Tao of nature brought all things into existence and governs their every action, not so much by force as by a kind of natural curvature in space and time."[17] Relativity also tells us that there is no universal flow of time, that different observers will see events occurring in different temporal sequences according to their respective positions and velocities, and that space and time are no longer homogeneous but heterogeneous. Let us now quote again Joseph Needham's remark that,

The assumption underlying the paradoxes (of the

Mohists) would therefore be that within the universal space–time continuum there are an infinitely large number of particular locations and particular times constantly changing their positions with regard to one another. From the standpoint of an observer at any one of them, the universe will look very different from that which another observer sees ... Its striking modernity ... invites one to wonder what Chinese science would have been capable of, without having to pass through the discipline of Aristotelian logic ...[18]

Equally important is physics' emphasis on the fact that all one can observe are *relations*; the Chinese always put all the emphasis on "relation" (*lien*) rather than substance which they did not take into consideration: "Where the Western minds asked '*what* essentially is it,' Chinese minds asked '*how* is it related in its beginnings, functions, and endings with everything else, and *how* ought we to react to it?' "[19]

Let us now recall Whitehead's saying that "The *event* is the unit of things real," and compare this statement with the doctrine of the *Avataṁsaka Sūtra*, the philosophical culmination of Indian Mahāyāna Buddhism. This work compares the universe to a vast network of crystals in which each crystal reflects all the others; this cosmic network is the Dharmadhātu, the universe itself which is made up of transient entities, *dharmas* or "thing-events." This doctrine, which acquired great importance in China under the T'ang dynasty, elaborates as follows the "Four Dharma Realms":

shih, the unique, individual thing-event of which the universe is made up.

li, the principle or ultimate reality underlying the multiplicity of thing-events.

li shi wu ai, which states that there is no obstruction between ultimate reality and thing-events.

shih shih wu ai, which adds that there is also no obstruction between the thing-events themselves, that is that every thing-event involves every other.[20]

Contemporary physics would concur that every "event" in the universe involves, more or less, every other. Physicist Ernst Mach rediscovered this fact when he put forth the "Mach Principle" according to which the inertia of any celestial body or system is dependent upon its interaction with all the rest of the universe (which prompted Einstein to postulate that the presence of matter and energy actually "curved" space–time). Each thing-event, according to the Dharmadhātu doctrine, is self-determinative, self-generating and spontaneous; the physical body of man, for instance, is a system of *shih shih wu ai* and ". . . a Buddha realizes that the whole universe is his body, a marvellously interrelated harmony organized from within itself rather than by interference from outside."[21] To this, the Hīnayāna schools of Buddhism add that all particles of being are not only perishable (*anitya*) but that their duration is infinitesimally short: "All things are as brief as a wink," (*yat sat tat kṣaṇikam*).[22]

Is the universe basically mental rather than material, as James Jeans asserts? The Mahāyāna school of philosophy known as Yogācāra agrees: the world of forms or thing-events is *cittamatra*, "mind only," or *vijñaptimatra*, "representation only."[23]

It is highly symbolic that such an eminent physicist as Erwin Schrödinger should lend his powerful voice to a persuasive defence of Eastern monism as against Western monotheism, in the light of the fundamental Oneness displayed at the microcosmic level of physics where all phenomena are interrelated and cannot be viewed as autonomous and isolated events or processes. He points out that the plurality perceived by us is an illusion, quoting Vedantic philosophy and its famous analogy of the universe assimilated to a many-faceted crystal which shows multitudes of pictures of what is a single reality, without multiplying it.[24] We have just seen that some schools of Mahāyāna Buddhism have used the same simile. He adds, in true Eastern fashion, that this has to be ". . . experienced, not simply given a notional acknowledgement."[25] While he refuses to accept Spinoza's pantheism, he claims that all conscious beings are "all in all' and that each one of our lives is not just a fragment of existence but, in a way, the *whole* of it—a whole constituted in such a way, however, that it cannot be seen at one glance.[26]

His basic theme is that consciousness is One and cannot be found in the plural, which plurality is an illusion. This illusion, in turn, triggered in Western philosophic thought a conflict between an inevitable idealism denying the existence of matter *à la* Berkeley and its complete uselessness in dealing with the objective physical world. He dismisses the conflict by referring specifically to one of the cardinal tenets of the *Upaniṣads* according to which the external world and consciousness are one and the same, being constituted of the same basic elements—which leads him to say that the fact that there is only *one* external world amounts to stating that there is only *one* consciousness.[27]

This ancient wisdom is not limited to the *Upaniṣads* and Vedānta. The Chinese Taoists long ago expressed the same monistic viewpoint; the *Tao Te Ching* states that "Therefore the sage embraces the Oneness (of the universe), making it his testing-instrument for everything under Heaven." Or we read in the *Kuan Tzu* book: "Only the *chün-tzu* (gentleman) holding to the idea of the One can bring about changes in things and affairs."[28]

This leads Schrödinger to abandon the dualism of thought and existence, or mind and matter.[29] This has been unsuccessfully attempted before in the West, although, as he remarks, ". . . it is odd that it has usually been done on a materialistic basis . . . But this is no good. If we decide to have only one sphere, it has got to be the psychic one, since that exists anyway."[30]

Another cardinal element is now introduced in this orientalization of the world-view of physics: the virtual disappearance of a sharp separation between object and subject, observer and thing observed, since the observer, like the mystic, is an active "participant" in the experiment and forms one whole with whatever is being observed.* Schrödinger, in sum, states that the reduction of the whole of reality to mental experience is itself an *idea*, a mental construction; he emphasizes, however, that he objects to the ". . . assertion that there must be also, externally to it or alongside it . . . an object of which it is the idea and by which it is caused."[31]

Here, as we see, he separates himself sharply from Einstein who still wanted to retain the object–subject dichotomy, that is the idea of the existence of a real objective universe independent of, and alongside, the human observer—an idea (metaphysical realism) which was already refuted, as we saw, by Heisenberg.

The monistic vision of the world, then, strips away the opposition subject–object, leaving the thinking and feeling subject, "consciousness," as the sole, ultimate reality. Schrödinger asserts that we must think that everything that happens takes place in our *experience* of it and that it requires no material substratum as the object of which it would be an experience—such substratum being completely superfluous.[32]

The scientific version of monism would then present itself as follows: according to Quantum Theory, while a given object—elementary particle, atom or whatever—can be divided into constituent parts, it does *not* actually consist of them; in other words, it is a whole whose presumed parts

* See James Jeans' statement on p. 28.

can be discovered only when its wholeness is destroyed. For instance, a neutron can disintegrate into a proton and an electron—true enough. But the very term "disintegrate" is actually incorrect, for it suggests that this neutron consists of the agglomeration of proton and electron, which it does not. This terminology is a remnant of the mechanistic outlook of the nineteenth century; and contemporary physicists would rather use the term "creation" in order to emphasize the fact that proton and electron do *not* pre-exist *in* the neutron: "Something *new* comes into existence which did not exist as such before."[33] Therefore, if we theoretically assimilate the whole universe to a vast quantum object, this universe does not consist of the multitude of objects—stars, planets, living beings—that populate it; it divides into such plurality ". . . only for those who look at it with a multifariously objectivizing point of view."[34]

In other words, nature itself exhibits a *holistic* tendency to form wholes that are greater than the sum of the parts we obtain when we break them up—a fact that was apprehended by the East thousands of years ago. From what kind of background does this *creative* evolution spring? Let us proceed a little further.

Without going so far as to endorse, as Schrödinger does, the connection between contemporary physics and Eastern metaphysics, many scientists have seen or felt that this new scientific vision has dealt a devastating blow to the traditional religious concepts of the West. Einstein, for instance, and in spite of Yahweh's ghost lurking in his cultural background, asserts that the root of the modern conflict between science and religion lies in the concept of a personal God; and that contemporary theologians should have the courage to reject it.[35] What is this except a plea to discard Western objectifying monotheism in favour of Eastern subjectifying monism? And to discard, once and for all, the anthropomorphism of the West? It is not that Einstein is in any sense anti-religious, quite the contrary; but his sense of religion comes much closer to the Oriental model than to the Occidental. He claims that what is important is the force of the super-personal content of religion and its overpowering meaningfulness, regardless of its possible link with a divinity; otherwise, neither Buddha nor Spinoza could be ranked as religious personalities.[36] And he concludes on the theme of the connection between science and religion: "It seems to me that science not only purifies the religious impulse of the dross of its anthropomorphism but also contributes to a religious spiritualization of our understanding of life[37] . . . Science without religion is lame, religion without science is blind."[38]

The cardinal fact is that contemporary physics finds a remarkable echo in Eastern, and not Western, metaphysics; and that one of the prime elements of this conjunction is the monistic, and not monotheistic, vision of underlying reality. Even Einstein who rejects monotheism but, paradoxically and incongruously, wants to retain its material counterpart in terms of the existence of a real physical universe independent of human consciousness, even he is, at heart, an Eastern monist, as are most scientists who are religiously inclined. One of the most indicative statements on this topic was penned by astrophysicist Fred Hoyle when he stated that all the Christianity offered him was an ". . . eternity of frustration." He strongly feels that life's main theme concerns the obvious inadequacy of one's own limited consciousness; and that, if free to choose, he would hope that our personal consciousness would merge with, or become welded to other individual consciousnesses to form a much greater super-personal structure. He believes that this dynamic evolution would be far more in keeping with the greatness of the universe ". . . than the static picture offered by formal religion."[39]

As for those agnostic Westerners who cling strictly to the objectifying form of philosophy while denying the objective God that goes with it, they find themselves in the pathetic predicament expressed by Bertrand Russell in his autobiography: "As regards metaphysics . . . I experienced the delight of believing that the sensible world is real. Bit by bit, chiefly under the influence of physics, this delight has faded, and I have been driven to a position not unlike that of Berkeley, without his God . . . I find myself involved in a vast mist of solitude both emotional and metaphysical, from which I can find no issue."[40] Indeed, within the strictly objectifying framework that is traditional in Western cultures, there is and can be *no* issue.

Let us recall Einstein's saying that there is no place in this new kind of physics for both the field and matter since the field is the only reality.* However, behind this field and its physical existence stands the mysterious and wholly non-material background, Eddington's "mind-stuff" or cosmic consciousness. We find something of this conceptual vision in all the traditional formulations of the East—the Void of the *Upaniṣads*, the Nirvāṇa of the Buddhists, the Tao of the Chinese—not quantified expressions of a science of physics but intuitively felt and seen with the mystical mind's inner eye—the Eye of Śiva in India's traditional lore. The void-like background postulated by physics (James Jeans' "substratum") which spontaneously produces and reabsorbs particles is thus essentially "creative potentiality"; it creates forms and destroys them; matter condenses out of it and disappears back into it. It is *śunya*, the Void of the Indians who, incidentally, out of this intuitive apprehension invented the mathematical symbol "zero" which the genius of the Greeks had never been able to conceive.

This Void is not emptiness, far from it; it is indeed creative potentiality, one which can presumably be experienced by mystical insight although science cannot penetrate beyond this ultimate barrier. The mystical emphasis is always put on the ultimate non-reality of the material world

* See p. 25.

and on the all-pervading reality of unindividualized consciousness (such as is postulated by the logical mind of Erwin
Schrödinger) which underlies all physical appearances—
but physical science can only stand on the threshold of this
"other side" or "beyond" of the visible universe. Can the
data of mystical insight and that of the sciences of nature
converge at some point?

8 CONVERGENCE

Traditional Eastern metaphysics and most Western biologists appear to agree on one main point—that life and the universe are pointless and purposeless. The classical Hindu and Buddhist outlook, anti-historic to the core, see no spiritual purpose in the universe and the gods will dance the world to destruction with the same cosmic pleasure they enjoyed when creating it. It is all a sport (*līlayā*) and creation is nothing more than a cosmic jest, a meaningless play whose stage is the universe of mental and material creation, and whose actors are illusionary gods and men. They all are a product of *māyā*, the phantasmal creation and deceptive display of forms through cosmic magic.[1]

To this, stripped of its mythology, the great majority of modern biologists would subscribe wholeheartedly. In spite of Whitehead's pithy remark that "Scientists who are animated by the purpose of proving that they are purposeless are an interesting subject for study,"[2] those scientists who attempt to see some goal or purpose in the world and in Evolution, are few. What is known as "vitalism" is very much of a minority report in the biological world where the great majority of scientists would rather level down than up—that is, adamantly refuse to extrapolate by looking upon the evolution of organic life on this planet as a meaningful process. In their view, mind and consciousness can only be epiphenomena of strictly material developments. In fact, if they could, many biologists would be glad to reduce biology to physics since they instinctively look upon living organisms as machines—very much as Descartes looked upon them, but without the autonomous reality of mind and soul which constituted the second half of his dualism.

Unfortunately, many of them do not seem to have grasped the philosophical implications of the revolution in contemporary physics.[3] Although they are intellectually aware of the new physics, they appear to feel an unconscious psychological compulsion—because of the much higher level of organized matter under their scrutiny—to deal with material "substances," however ultimately non-existent they may be in the eye of the physicist. Many biologists are still unconsciously Victorian in their philosophic assumptions.

Our guide in this brief survey of some of the philosophical implications of physics that were not touched upon previously, will be the famous physicist Max Planck, author of the revolutionary Quantum Theory. Max Planck points out that one of the fundamental laws ruling the physical world specifies that, of all the processes that will take a closed system from one state to another in a given time framework, the one that will actually take place will be the process whose integer for that time framework will be the smallest—integer known as the function of Lagrange. If one knows the expression of that function, it will be easy to determine completely the development of the process before it even takes place.[4] This law, known as the principle of minimum action, reintroduces another form of causality already analyzed by Aristotle: instead of an *efficient* cause that starts from the present in order to determine future effects, we now have a *final* cause which proceeds in reverse fashion by ascribing to a specific goal the cause of the development that leads to it.[5] What this implies of course, is that "Theoretical physics," in Planck's own words, "has reached a kind of causality with a definite teleological character, without it contradicting in the least natural scientific laws." And he adds that this law "cannot help awaken in unbiased minds the feeling that nature is ruled by a rational will aiming at a specific goal." [6]

This has far-reaching implications. Recent work by scientists suggests that some "advance-time" solutions in physics, which are usually discarded, in fact correspond to successions of events converging toward some form of finality. Physicist Costa de Beauregard claims that ". . . although such events are generally observable on the gross level of everyday life, the finality principle is expected to be maximally operative in just those situations where consciousness intrudes as an ordering phenomenon." [7]

In their joint work, *The Interpretation of Nature and the Psyche*, physicist Wolfgang Pauli and psychologist Carl Jung tell us that if natural law were absolute, there could be no deviation from it. But since efficient causality is only a *statistical* truth, there is plenty of scope for exceptions. Jung regards synchronistic events as precisely the acausal exceptions allowed for by statistical law—they are more or less independent of space and time in the sense that space does not interfere with their occurrence, and that the time sequence can be inverted so that one may actually perceive an event that has not yet occurred. This possibility is confirmed by the fact that quantum field theory states that the simplest definition of antiparticles is that of particles moving *backward* in time. What gives, at the human level, the impression that time invariably moves forward in one direction from past to future is the statistical fact of the gigantic preponderance (in our part of the universe) of particles over antiparticles. [8]

Another paranormal but relatively frequent phenomenon, the ability to see instantaneously an event occurring thousands of miles away, can be hypothetically explained by the possibility that information can be carried instantaneously by extremely low frequency electromagnetic waves. But many physicists now incline to think that these phenomena have to be explained at the level of quantum physics within the framework of the impact of observation on physical experiments. What is known as "quantum interconnected-ness" attempts to link far distant events in a mathematical scheme known as Bell's Theorem—distant entities in the universe can apparently act as parts of a greater whole.[9]

Max Planck thus reintroduces a teleological element in the universe which he ascribes to a non-physical spiritual entity. He states that in order to designate that reality, religion uses its own symbols, while science discovers it on the horizon of its calculations based on the testimony of our sense-perceptions. Nothing, therefore, prevents us from identifying these two powers that remain equally mysterious for us, the order of the world as determined by the sciences of nature and the God of religion.[10] He sees no incompatibility between science and religion; on the contrary, he sees a *convergence* on essential points. The great difference between the two, however, is that for the religious man, God is a fact given at once and prior to everything else, whereas, for the scientist, the prior data is the content of sensorial perceptions and the calculations drawn from them: for religion God is at the beginning of thought, for science He is reached at the end.[11]

In reintroducing teleology, Max Planck mentions that it can be applied to the science of biology,[12] which would make it into a "biology of purpose," as one biologist has put it. Biology is the science of the nature of life and the introduction of purpose in the development of organic entities. implies that man, for instance, reaches out for goals that are built into his own character and physiology; in which case, the living organism is not to be analyzed in terms of where it comes from but of where it is going. A definite pattern or norm directs its development, whether physical or supraphysical. This implies that organic matter is not completely comprehensible in terms of efficient causality and cannot be understood in mere physico-chemical terms.

The new physics tell us why. One of the ultimate consequences of Heisenberg's Principle of Indeterminacy is that the basic structure of living matter lies below the threshold of its "indeterminacy." At the turn of the century, it was still possible to believe in the natural extension of physical and mechanical determinism to organic as well as to inorganic matter, and to believe that living matter was just a more complex form of physical organization such as a computer, but obeying the same ironclad laws as dead matter. And if, by chance, atoms and molecules behaved differently in living organisms, it should be possible to find a strictly physico-chemical interpretation for it.

Quantum mechanics now explain to us the complete meaninglessness of such a viewpoint: the greater our knowledge about the state of the atoms inside a living organism, the greater the disturbance caused by the act of observation and measurement. Werner Heisenberg has pointed out with Niels Bohr that "It may well be that a description of the living organism that could be called complete from the standpoint of the physicist cannot be given, since it would require experiments that interfere too strongly with the biological functions."[13] For example, let us take the smallest living entity, a virus; this virus can only be seen through an electron microscope—but since the virus cannot possibly survive the bombardment of electrons, all we can see is a dead, lifeless virus—a virus deprived of that one quality we want to study scientifically, its life.[14] Schrödinger clinches the matter by reminding us that ". . . incredibly small groups of atoms, much too small to display exact statistical laws, do play a dominating role in the very orderly and lawful events within a living organism. They have control of the observable large-scale features which the organism acquires in the course of its development."[15] The gap between organic and inorganic matter therefore, cannot be spanned.

Niels Bohr, short of bridging it, has attempted to deal with this gap by extending to the relationship between physics and biology his own strictly physical Theory of Complementarity which sets up, on the basis of Quantum Theory, parallel and complementary frames of reference, each with its own laws but which are not derivable from one another. He therefore suggests a similar complementarity between living organisms and lifeless matter, each system being autonomous with its own specific rules and laws—which would, of course, imply the impossibility of reducing life to a strict physico-chemical system. He points out that,

> The existence of life must be considered as an elementary fact that cannot be explained, but must be taken as a starting point in biology, in a similar way as the quantum of action, which appears as an irrational element from the point of view of classical mechanical physics, taken together with the existence of elementary particles, forms the foundation of atomic physics.[16]

In this context, it would therefore appear that both efficient and final causalities are one and the same mental explanation—the former one being an intellectual device for the understanding of lifeless, inorganic matter, the latter for the goal-directed behaviour of organic matter and life in general, from protoplasm to man—both obviously operating within the individual organism, reconciling mechanism and teleology, that would determine our understanding of physiological as well as psychological purpose from the growth of a cell to the work of the human mind. Again, Niels Bohr points out that,

> These two ways of looking at things are contradictory. For in the first case we assume that an event is determined by the purpose it serves, by its goal. In the second case we believe that an event is determined by its immediate predecessor. It seems most unlikely that both approaches should have led to the same result by pure chance. In fact, they complement each other, and, as we

have long since realized, both are correct precisely because there is such a thing as life. Biology thus has no need to ask which of the two viewpoints is the more correct, but only how nature managed to arrange things so that the two should fit together.[17]

Living matter's most characteristic feature is that it maintains definite patterns, and that these patterns shape its growth into distinct organisms in such a way that no simple physico-chemical explanation can account for it. More significant still, in the living activity of organic matter, it is not the specific character of its constituents but the *relations* between them that is important—reminding us of the "organismic" world-outlook of the Chinese.* For instance, the egg of a frog at the beginning of its development divides into two cells which, if artificially separated, grow, each of them, into a *whole* individual instead of only half a one—implying that the development of each cell is different from what it would have been, had it been allowed to remain in a two-cell embryo.[18] This would be rather difficult to explain on a pure physico-chemical basis!

Unlike dead, inorganic matter, an organism is an *organized* system in which each part is related in a specific way to the whole, aiming at a certain peak of development while maintaining along the way a state of delicate balance of function that will automatically attempt to re-establish itself if altered. Thus, an organism is not so much an aggregate of cells as an *architecture*, a dynamic whole that is far more than the sum of its parts—here again, nature displays its "holistic" tendency. The visible expression of its organizing activity is its *form* which owes nothing to chance but appears to be the goal toward which its organic development strives.

A living organism is a remarkably delicate and unstable piece of architecture, however. It is an "open" system which absorbs and rejects material continuously in an effort

* See p.166

to maintain fairly constant conditions within itself in order to be in a "steady state." This is exactly what life is, with death as the inevitable result of its disruption. It is a plain fact that if an organism is blocked in its attempt to reach its "norm" in the usual way, it will try to reach it some other way: here we do see "final" causation in action; the end rather than the means is the important thing.

To sum up, organization is primarily a result of relations which are impossible to explain in strictly physical terms; this relational function on which the Chinese world-picture was based does not fit well into the traditional Western outlook, which is why biologists have tried to focus on *substances*, that is to look for physical, and more especially chemical, explanations, but with little success so far. It is rather the biophysicists who have put forth the most fruitful suggestions by positing the existence of "formative fields" or bioelectric fields enveloping and penetrating or suffusing organisms and controlling their development—suggestions which they state in terms of field physics rather than particles. Neurophysiologists have discovered that the electrical pathways of the nerves appear to develop *before* the growth of the nervous tissue itself; the implication being that they would constitute formative fields pre-existing the nervous matter and guiding its development.[19] The Kirlian technique is now capable of photographing energies and auras surrounding organic bodies—energies which are not located *in* the body but of which the substantial body itself would be a sort of "condensation." At any rate, the problem of "form," "pattern" or *organization* appears to be the fundamental one and Joseph Needham is probably correct in stating that "Organization and Energy are the two fundamental problems which all science has to solve."[20]

Implicit in organization is *purpose*; and more than one biologist has drawn attention to the close connection between physiological and psychological developments, especially to their common directiveness which "... is shown equally well in the development of the embryo as in our own conscious behaviour. It is this directive activity shown by individual organisms that distinguishes living things from inanimate objects."[21] Purpose is therefore an intimate part of organic nature and is not arbitrarily "imported" into it; goal-directed processes of development of both physiological and psychological life are complementary sets of activity which point to a real psychophysical unity—one of the basic concepts of the Eastern outlook.

The existence of a relationship between biology and psychology in the sense of a relation between organic development and psychological purpose appears to be an inevitable conclusion. It appears to be both an *objective* fact of biology observable in the laboratory; and also a *subjective* psychological fact which we can all observe for ourselves *in* ourselves: everyone of our mental activities and decisions is goal-oriented, otherwise we could not live. The purely instinctive development of an embryo and the conscious purpose originating in the infinitely complex activities of the brain would therefore be the two sides of the same coin: life–purpose. Both are basically biological phenomena, although the higher we rise in the hierarchic complexities of individual organisms, the greater the part played by the nervous system—which is lacking in the realms of vegetals and the lowest animals. Henri Bergson, however, has convincingly explained that rudimentary consciousness does not have to involve the actual presence of a nervous system; this system merely crystallizes and channels in a definite direction and according to a definite pattern a rudimentary activity which is widely diffused in all organic substances, and brings it up to a much higher pitch of intensity.[22] All organic material displays, in an imperfect way, a certain resemblance to nervous tissue; the latter would thus be an increasingly specialized kind of tissue which emerged during the course of Evolution.

Here, we can see at work the conjunction of objective

outlook and subjective insight due to the evident fact that we are all *inside* a highly complex living organism. Obviously, the biologist has a much more intimate knowledge of his material because "... he himself is that sample."[23] This subjective insight grants him a kind of knowledge that is inaccessible to the scientist who looks at it objectively from the outside. He has, therefore, two completely different tools to work with, one of which is provided by the fact that he is himself a biological entity. Understandably, scientists have been reluctant to attempt to incorporate such subjective data because of the difficulty in analyzing and measuring the results of direct insight.

At any rate, it becomes clear that, rather than analyze organic entities strictly in terms of matter and energy, which is the dream of many biologists who would reduce their science to physico-chemical explanations, the reverse might ultimately be more likely—that "... life, as a very special category of the physical universe, may in time make contributions of its own to our knowledge of matter and energy."[24] As the brilliant biochemist and geneticist J. B. S. Haldane points out,

> As the conception of organism is a higher and more concrete conception than that of matter and energy, science must ultimately aim at gradually interpreting the physical world of matter and energy in terms of the biological conception of organism.[25]

This would go further than Niels Bohr's suggestion of two different and "complementary" outlooks on the physical universe by giving biology a priority over physics; as one scientist put it, "The notions of physics will have to be enriched, and this enrichment will come from biology."[26] Physics itself has paved the way and left an opening for such a possibility. Arthur Eddington explains that,

> ... the distinction between ordinary matter and conscious matter is that in ordinary matter there is no correla-

tion in the undetermined parts of the behaviour of the particles, whereas in conscious matter correlation may occur. Such correlation is looked upon as an interference with the ordinary course of nature, due to the association of consciousness with the matter; in other words, it is the physical aspect of volition.[27]

This clearly indicates that the root of consciousness is wholly beyond what we term physical nature, that is the space–time universe that our senses apprehend, and that *consciousness is related to life as meaning is to expression.* Consciousness intrudes into our space–time universe by means of organic developments, but springs from another dimension altogether, coming, as it were, from inside out. Consciousness, as such, is deathless since it belongs to a plane of reality that is beyond life and death as well as beyond time and space—death being merely the withdrawal of consciousness from the space–time universe of phenomena that we can observe from outside; what dies and is reborn, however, is the *expression* of consciousness, that is organic life.

This being the case, it is obvious that the mysterious spiritual force which appears to sustain life and consciousness, and which the mystic appears to apprehend in his ecstatic experiences, would have to be brought into play and, up to a certain point, *objectified*, and brought within the conspectus of science. How is this to be done and where is the scientifically-minded mystic who can point the way?

Early one morning in December 1937, a thirty-four-year-old Kashmiri Brahmin sat cross-legged in a small cell-like room in the city of Jammu, located in northern India; he was meditating deeply, as he had done for many years. Early in life, an essentially well-balanced and rational-minded agnostic who was as keenly disappointed by the teachings of traditional Hinduism as by the apparent materialism of the scientific outlook, he decided to search on his own without the usual assistance of a *guru*. Seventeen years of regular meditation went by and, disappointingly, nothing happened ... until that fateful December of 1937: this time, the experience proved to be dramatically different. At first, it was no more than an odd feeling of something moving below the base of the spine, strong enough however to interrupt his meditation. The sensation disappeared and he resumed his meditation. Stronger than before, the sensation recurred, became stronger and stronger, and,

> Suddenly, with a roar like that of a waterfall, I felt a stream of liquid light entering my brain through the spinal cord ... The illumination grew brighter and brighter, the roaring louder and louder, I experienced a rocking sensation and then felt myself slipping out of my body, entirely enveloped in a halo of light. It is impossible to describe the experience accurately. I felt the point of consciousness that was myself growing wider and wider, spreading outward while the body, normally the immediate object of its perception, appeared to have receded into the distance until I became entirely unconscious of it. I was now all consciousness, without any outline, without any idea of a corporeal appendage, without any feeling or sensation coming from the senses, immersed in a sea of light, simultaneously conscious and aware of every point, spread out as it were, in all directions without any barrier or material obstruction. I was no longer myself, or to be more accurate, no longer as I knew myself to be, a small point of awareness confined in a body, but instead was a vast circle of consciousness in which the body was but a point, bathed in light and in a state of exhaltation and happiness impossible to describe.[28]

Thus started one of the most incredible spiritual odysseys of the twentieth century. Twelve gruelling years were going to pass before Pandit Gopi Krishna, the hero of this metaphysical adventure, found himself again in this state of ecstatic bliss. Quite unprepared, either intellectually or physically, for this adventure in transcendental realms, he underwent the tortures of the damned and literally descended into the bowels of a Dantean hell. This continuous stream of liquid light turned into a kind of nightmarish flame-thrower, burning and scorching his insides in the midst of roaring sounds and terrifying inner lights. There appeared to be no relief from the devastating current rising ceaselessly from the seat of *kuṇḍalinī*.[29] He began to fear that he was on the verge of insanity. His body wasted away, he could no longer eat and lost all desire to live, so intense was his suffering, by night as by day. The internal blasting increased steadily, ". . . blistering the organs and tissues like flying sparks."[30]

He finally made up his mind to commit suicide. But it then occurred to him, being a technically-minded man, that he might have accidentally aroused *kuṇḍalinī* through the hot solar channel, *pingala*, rather than through the *suṣumṇā* within the spine, as he should have. He decided, by a supreme effort of the will, to attempt to shift the implacable current to the cool lunar channel, *ida*, on the left side, to counteract the horrifying fire that was raging inside. Applying all the mental concentration he could muster into picturing in his mind the traditional tantric diagram, he did so. The result was astounding: "There was a sound like a nerve thread snapping and instantaneously a silvery streak passed zigzag through the spinal cord . . . filling my head with a blissful lustre in place of the flame that had been tormenting me."[31]

His first ordeal was over, but there were several others to come and each was overcome, not only by his indomitable willpower but by his growing understanding of the mysterious force that was operating within him. In a sense, his body and physiological apparatus became his own laboratory, and each error in his mental and physical behaviour became a source of increasing knowledge of the intimate connection between his physiology and his mystical experiences. He began to realize that this uncanny force was gradually remoulding his psycho-physiological apparatus so as to enable to it stand the intense strain of his state of higher consciousness. Baffled by this amazing metamorphosis of his inner being, he wrote to the greatest living Indian saint at the time, Śrī Aurobindo in far-away Pondicherry, detailing his experiences. In reply, Aurobindo confirmed that there was no doubt that he had aroused *kuṇḍalinī* the Tantric way and that he should seek out a competent *yogī* to help him; but none was available. He had to go on, struggling alone, and struggle alone he did.

In the process, he soon came to some philosophic conclusions of great importance, which he held to all the more firmly because he was actually *living* them. He literally saw *through* earthly life and behind it, perceived the existence of a kind of cosmic super-intelligence using organic compounds as an architect uses his materials. He became convinced that life and Evolution were not the haphazard results of chance or undesigned occurrences but were, on the contrary, products of purposeful and deliberate cosmic design.[32]

Meantime, the struggle went on and so did his psychosomatic observations. He began to feel that he had been destined by this transcendental and vital intelligent medium to undergo these traumatic experiences in order to communicate them to the world at large, but mostly stripped of the traditional symbolism and mythology of the East.

Finally, after many years of struggle and suffering, he quite suddenly reached the trans-human stage of permanent rapturous insight (*samādhi*) in which he still is at this writing. He had, in fact and at last, reached the truly contemplative state where, with the laser-like insight of the

Eye of Śiva, he could look at the physical universe from the "other side," so to speak. His descriptions of it are worth quoting at length since they appear to provide the most clinically detailed picture of that mystical state in our century; it is as if he had actually gone through the "event horizon" of an astronomical Black Hole:

> ... I stopped abruptly, contemplating with awe and amazement, which made the hair on my skin stand on end, a marvellous phenomenon in progress in the depths of my being[33] ... I had expanded in an indescribable manner into a titanic personality, conscious from within of an immediate and direct contact with an intensely conscious universe, a wonderful inexpressible immanence all around me[34] ... The phenomenal world ... receded into the background and assumed the appearance of an extremely thin, rapidly melting layer of foam upon a substantial rolling ocean of life, a veil of exceedingly fine vapour before an infinitely large conscious sun, constituting a complete reversal of the relationship between the world and the limited human consciousness. It showed the previously all-dominating cosmos reduced to the state of a transitory appearance and the ... point of awareness, circumscribed by the body, grown to the spacious dimensions of a mighty universe and the exalted stature of a majestic immanence before which the material cosmos shrank to the subordinate position of an evanescent and illusive appendage.[35]

Thus, probably, was the concept of illusory *māyā* born, thousands of years ago, and with it the whole metaphysical outlook of the East.[36] It is no wonder that in the Orient, time and again, the accomplished *yogī* was tempted to forget the space–time world altogether and plunge forever into this rapturous "beyond." Only a strong sense of mission, that prophetic instinct so much more alive in Western tradition than in the ahistorical East, can compel the mystic to remain on earth in order to communicate his insight. Having reached *samādhi*, Śrī Rāmakrishna had to pull himself together, crying to himself, "come down, come down!" in order to continue his mission on earth; and he pleaded: "O Mother, let me not attain these delights, let me remain in my normal state, so that I can be of more use to the world."[37] Swāmī Vivekānanda, his chosen disciple, while less mystically endowed, was almost induced by a famous *yogī*, Pavhari Baba of Gazipur, to forsake the world as well as the mission entrusted to him by Rāmakrishna and follow him in the ecstatic delights of total and permanent contemplation: Pavhari Baba stated many times that work is bondage and that the spirit alone, without earthly activity, could help other men.[38] The concept of Christian charity and love, on the other hand, often helped the Western mystic resist the lure. The great Ruysbroeck himself said that "... if you are ravished in ecstasy as highly as St. Peter or St. Paul or as anybody you like, and if you hear that a sick man is in need of hot soup, I counsel you to wake up from your ecstasy and warm the soup for him. Leave God to serve God: find Him and serve Him in His members: you will lose nothing by the change."[39]

One of the marked features of Pandit Gopi Ḳrishna's experiences was the brutal impact of these ecstasies on his relatively delicate physiological apparatus and the bouts of sickness they caused. The silver lining in this cloud was the fact that he was able to understand the close connection between physiology and mental states, which would not have been so obvious otherwise.[40] He gradually developed his theory of purposeful Evolution of the human race from primordial times to the contemporary world and became convinced that what he experienced in his transcendental states was merely a prefiguration of mankind's next development in terms of expanded consciousness. Thus, to him, religion in its mystical expression is merely the outward expression of the evolutionary impulse.[41]

This brings us to the crux of the matter: can a connection between the scientific and mystical frames of reference be established over and beyond a certain metaphysical parallelism? The answer lies perhaps in the fact that Indian mysticism, at least as far as its leading representatives are concerned, has evolved as much in the past hundred years as the science of physics itself, in a direction that points toward an inevitable convergence of the two. From its modern awakening with Śrī Rāmakrishna and Swāmī Vivekānanda, Eastern mysticism has begun to adapt its revelations to the entirely different cultural framework provided by science and technology, without in any way sacrificing what is valid in its traditional understanding of the phenomenon itself. The true departure occurred with the life and writings of Śrī Aurobindo who began to weld India's traditional metaphysics to the concept of a modified and purposeful Evolution—quite a departure for the offspring of a culture that had consistently ignored the spiritual significance of time and history.

Śrī Aurobindo, whose cosmic optimism embraced the whole of Evolution from distant past to remote future, became convinced that the coming of "super-man" was as certain as the coming of man before the appearance of mankind, and that his progress from mind to super-mind would be as revolutionary as the progress of unconscious life to conscious mind. But he did more than proclaim this advent; as is traditional in the East, he was also a mystic who experimented with himself and expounded a philosophy of transformation rather than intellectual information. In reply to a disciple's query, he once stated: "What you call thinking, I never do. I see or I don't see. That is all."[42] His total being was involved in the search for the processes whereby such a new type of man could arise, and undoubtedly felt himself to be the mystical spearhead of

Evolution itself, as if thousands of years of spiritual quest in the East, liberating the Self of the devotee who escaped into transcendental spheres but did little for his fellow-men, was now going to be deflected toward the "socialization" of spiritual achievement and its extension to mankind at large, so that through a reshaping of matter, life and mind, an entirely new spiritualized way of life could prevail on this planet.

Long ago, with the advent of humanity came the birth of reflection in the human animal who not only thinks, but knows that he thinks. From then on man could reflect the universe in his own mind, remember the past and foresee the future, and direct his own evolution. In one gigantic leap, humanity outstripped mere life, as the super-man of the future will outstrip mere man. Just as man was not merely a new animal species but a *new form of life*, the future's super-man will embody an entirely new type of thought and being. Just as thoughtful, reflective man represented an "interiorization" of the individual converging upon himself, the future's super-man will symbolize the convergence of mankind upon itself—a thickening film of humanity covering the planet's surface which, having reached the limits of its spatial extension and diversification that had stretched, time-wise, through the Palaeolithic, the Neolithic and historical times, is now reaching saturation point and will henceforth have to progress in another dimension: the deepening of its consciousness, a collective interiorization of humanity as a whole, in order to counteract the centrifugal tendencies that threaten contemporary mankind. The leader in the process will have to be this new type of man.

In *The Ideal of Human Unity*, Aurobindo clearly defined the future perspective in religious terms: "The fundamental idea is that mankind is the godhead to be worshipped and served by man and that the respect, the service, the progress of the human being and human life are the chief duty and chief aim of the human spirit."[43] But he warns and questions ". . . whether a purely intellectual and sentimental religion of humanity will be sufficient to bring about so great a change in our psychology," since ". . . it does not get at the centre of man's being. The intellect and the feelings are only instruments of the being . . ."[44] It only remains to conclude, in Aurobindo's words, that the goal can be secured "when founded upon a change of the inner human nature and inner way of living," leading to a "larger inward life."[45] And he adds: "The unity of the human race . . . can only be secured and can only be made real if the religion of humanity, which is at present the highest active ideal of mankind, spiritualizes itself and becomes the general inner law of human life."[46]

In other words, this new religious mode must not only be thought out intellectually, but must be experienced and actually *lived*—obviously, in the beginning, by a small number of exceptional men drawn from all over the world, from every nationality and every living culture. Multidimensional men will then become the living embodiment of the great synthesis—synthesis between the most profound psychological insights provided by traditional religions and the most recent findings of depth psychology and biochemistry. In one of his most eloquent passages, Aurobindo emphasizes that India ". . . must send forth from herself the future religion of the entire world, the Eternal religion which is to harmonize all religions, science and philosophies and make mankind one soul."[47]

The experiences and theories of Gopi Krishna simply extend, but in bold and revolutionary fashion, this historical trend. If Aurobindo was the poet of the future, he is the technician. For the first time, he has presented the mystical experience in slightly surrealistic terms, but stripped of most of the traditional symbolism and mythology that has always enwrapped it in both the East and the West. It is understandable that a man of such calibre feels that his incredible ordeals and suffering and finally triumph must have a meaning, and that this meaning endows him with an obligation: to transmit a message to the world, but a special type of message that would, for the first time, be subject to scientific scrutiny. So that a prophetic warning is sounded, probably equal in historical importance to Buddha's teaching, twenty-five hundred years ago; but not a dogmatic prophecy in the style of the Hebrews, the Gospels or the Koran; rather pointers and indicators to assist future scientific research. It is thanks to the great number of acute somatic observations which he made on himself during the course of his inner transformations, that he has been able to analyze clinically his bodily sensations and mental experiences and draw some tentative conclusions.

He claims, on the basis of his personal experiences, that it is not possible to fully apprehend Ultimate Reality *at the present stage of Evolution*—this Ultimate Reality still being at an immense distance from contemporary man, even when he is in the transhuman state of the fully evolved mystic. What he can achieve, at the present stage in history, is entrance into a new dimension of consciousness in which the *objective* world more or less disappears as such, to become unmistakably a *projection* of human consciousness.[48]

On the face of it, he appears to deny the exhalted claims of the East as to an identification-fusion with the Divinity, at this stage of Evolution at least, but without endorsing either the anthropomorphic idea of a personal God. His metaphysical views remain anchored in the concrete experience of his own psychosomatic states, as observed during his own mystical transformations.

Gopi Krishna claims, on the basis of those observations, that the same impulse that provides the mystic with his spiritual insights also underlies the whole process of mankind's Evolution—in other words, that we may have to deal in this instance with a mysterious spiritual law that would *also* be a biological law. If this be true, here would be at least one hinge between science and mysticism that could be partly amenable to the objectifying process of science. Very much like the study of traces left by elementary particles in cloud chambers, the physiological traces in the body left by the mystical experience could possibly be scientifically observed and analysed. As already pointed out earlier, no one has ever actually *seen* an electron, just as no one can *see* a mystical ecstasy in another human being without undergoing the experience himself—but in both cases, the "traces," the indirect evidence provided by the "inferential" data, are amenable to scientific treatment.

In order to present his thesis, he has recourse to two fundamental concepts provided by India's traditional metaphysics: *prāṇa* and *kuṇḍalinī*. *Prāṇa* (*ch'i*, in Chinese) is conceived as the all-pervading life element which appears on the borderline between the material and the non-material, part physical, part *meta*physical. He asserts, on the basis of his experiences, that it is all at once the "nourishment" of expanding consciousness and *also* the all-pervasive, life-inducing energy pouring out of a cosmic intelligence shaping the evolution of all living matter according to a mysterious but deliberate and purposeful design. This, of course, is a reaffirmation of the concept of teleology or final cause, which appears to contradict the purposelessness or "chance" element in the Darwinian theory of natural selection, as well as the traditional Indian concept of purposeless *līlayā*; but it confirms Max Planck's own teleological assertion. Gopi Krishna does not hesitate to claim that mankind's Evolution is basically determined by its goal, and that this goal is the achievement of higher consciousness by man in the future.

What can physics say about such a bold concept as *prāṇa* which springs straight out of Eastern mystical insight? Modern physics sees nothing incompatible between *prāṇa* and present-day scientific insight; in fact, since *prāṇa* is essentially "moving potency," a vitalizing principle, it could possibly be assimilated to Quantum Theory's "prob-

ability amplitude."[49] Physicist Weizsäcker terms probability a "futuristic concept," that is the quantified expression of the goal toward which the "flow of time" is
attempting to evolve—Bergson's "Elan Vital." This Elan
Vital splits into multitudes of human beings, each with its
own objective consciousness; the implication is that the
dualism object–subject prevails only as an approximation to
reality, an approximation thanks to which human beings
can objectivize, for practical purposes, what belongs essentially and ultimately to the subject.[50]

We have, again, reached a frontier beyond which objectification can no longer proceed. Within these limits, however, objectification can proceed indefinitely. With the twin
concepts of *prāṇa* and "probability amplitude," the *subject*
is reintroduced as being increasingly identified with the
fundamental "real," while the validity of objectification
still obtains as long as we remain in the realm of the sciences of nature. The biological assimilation of *prāṇa* to the
hypothetical "formative fields" or bioelectric fields mentioned earlier, is also a tantalizing possibility.

As for *kuṇḍalinī*, it appears to be the evolutionary
potency itself, closely connected with sublimated sexual
potency, which appears to be present in all human beings to
a greater or lesser extent. Hosts of new questions are raised
by this Eastern interpretation of a fundamental psychosomatic phenomenon. For instance, it is evident that scientific research must focus on what actually happens in the
reproductive system to cause sexual sublimation, as well as
on its connection with mental creativity. It appears to be a
well-established fact that the average man uses only a frac-
tion of his brain capacity; could it be that this sexual sublimation, triggering the rise of this potent force, actually puts
to use part or whole of this unused brain capacity? In any
case, *kuṇḍalinī* does not have to awaken as explosively as it
did in Gopi Krishna's case, and can very well "drip" slowly
upwards, stopping short of the true mystical experience but

endowing its possessor with unusual creative powers. It is also clear that his ghastly flirtation with insanity has given Gopi Krishna a new insight into the problem of the well-known closeness between genius and madness—the latter being the possible result of this immensely powerful force having been misdirected and having arisen through the wrong channel. Under one name or another, in any case, this fiery current appears to awaken and rise in all mystical illuminations—Pascal's "fire," for instance—and the physiological repercussions of this arousing of the Tantric "Serpent Power" might well be analyzable by medical science.

It is Gopi Krishna's claim, which parallels Aurobindo's, that while our normal present-day form of self-consciousness may have appeared sporadically in our anthropoid ancestors, only to become the norm today, hundreds of thousands of years later, the higher stages of consciousness provided by the awakening of this mysterious force, which appears only occasionally here and there in mystics and geniuses, will become the norm of the future for the whole human race. If and when this happens, all present-day institutionalized religions and denominations will melt away like butter under the sun. Blind faith will no longer be required because it will be replaced by *knowledge*—man will actually open the inner Eye of Śiva that is closed in most of us and live in a permanent transcendental state, in a spiritual reality that will be as self-evident to him as are his thoughts and sensorial perceptions today. He will see, hear, touch and taste the truth that lies beyond the space–time world. Death will hold no more terrors for him and he will become a deliberate participant in the great task of raising human consciousness to ever higher levels, fulfilling the Nietzschean Zarathustra's prophetic claim: "I teach you the Superman. Man is something that is to be overcome."

It might well be that mankind is now on the threshold of a psychological and physiological revolution of a magnitude that will overshadow all the social and political revolutions of our century—made possible by the seemingly incongruous, yet perfectly logical marriage between science and Eastern mysticism's insights.

NOTES AND REFERENCES

Chapter 1   SCIENCE AND RELIGION

1. Eddington, *The Nature of the Physical World*, p. 344.
2. Jeans, *Physics and Philosophy*, p. 126.
3. *Albert Einstein, Philosopher–Scientist*, ed. P. A. Schilpp, p. 551.
4. Heisenberg, *Physics and Beyond*, p. 88.
5. Barnett, *The Universe and Dr. Einstein*, p. 93.
6. Ibid., p. 112.
7. Ibid., p. 22.
8. Jeans, *Physics and Philosophy*, p. 169.
9. Capek, *The Philosophical Impact of Contemporary Physics*, p. 319.
10. Ford, *Elementary Particles*, p. 215.
11. Koestler, *The Roots of Coincidence*, p. 57.
12. Jeans, *Physics and Philosophy*, p. 169.
13. Sullivan, *The Limitations of Science*, p. 141.
14. Heisenberg, *Physics and Beyond*, p. 104.
15. Eddington, *The Nature of the Physical World*, p. 255.
16. Reichenbach, *The Rise of Scientific Philosophy*, pp. 183–5.
17. Jeans, *Physics and Philosophy*, p. 127.
18. Ibid., p. 169.
19. Ibid., p. 175.
20. Ibid., p. 172.
21. Eddington, *The Nature of the Physical World*, p. 290.
22. Heisenberg, *Physics and Philosophy*, p. 132.

23. Tresmontant, *Comment se pose Aujourd'hui le Problème de l'Existence de Dieu*, p. 357.
24. Sullivan, *The Limitations of Science*, p. 145.
25. Jeans, *The Mysterious Universe*, p. 137.
26. Quoted in Sullivan, *The Limitations of Science*, p. 144.
27. Eddington, *The Nature of the Physical World*, p. 332.
28. Wigner, *Symmetries and Reflexions*, p. 172.
29. Eddington, *The Nature of the Physical World*, p. 277.
30. Ibid., p. 282.
31. Ibid., p. 323.
32. Heisenberg, *Physics and Beyond*, p. 84.
33. Eddington, *The Nature of the Physical World*, p. 350.
34. Quoted in Coulson, *Science and Christian Belief*, pp. 27–8.
35. Quoted in Ibid., p. 33.
36. Quoted in Ibid., p. 41.
37. Quoted in Ibid., p. 18.
38. Eliade, *Yoga, Immortality and Freedom*, p. 151.
39. Dante, *The Divine Comedy*, p. 605.
40. Bourke, *Aquinas' Search for Wisdom*, pp. 192–3.
41. *The Gospel of Ramakrishna*, ed. Swami Nikhilananda, pp. 645–6.
42. Quoted in Frank, *Einstein*, pp. 340–1.
43. Schrödinger, *My View of the World*, p. 19.

Chapter 2 THE MAGIC MIND

1. *The Tibetan Book of the Great Liberation*, ed. Evans–Wentz, p. XLV.
2. Frankfort, *Before Philosophy*, p. 12.
3. Lévi-Strauss, *La Pensée Sauvage*, p. 3.
4. Campbell, *The Masks of God: Primitive Mythology*, p. 21.
5. Frankfort, *Before Philosophy*, p. 13.
6. Ibid., p. 14.

7. Needham, *Science and Civilization in China*, vol. 2, p. 284.
8. Frankfort, *Before Philosophy*, p. 21.
9. Frazer, *The Golden Bough*, p. 41.
10. Frankfort, *Before Philosophy*, p. 30.
11. Bastide, *Les Problèmes de la Vie Mystique*, pp. 25–9.
12. Underhill, *Mysticism*, p. 70.

Chapter 3 EAST AND WEST

1. *The Tibetan Book of the Great Liberation*, ed. Evans–Wentz, p. 12.
2. Schrödinger, *What is Life?*, p. 184.
3. Radhakrishnan, *Indian Philosophy*, vol. 2, p. 506.
4. Ibid., vol. 1, p. 185.
5. Ibid., vol. 1, p. 155.
6. Quoted in Needham, *Science and Civilization in China*, vol. 2, p. 303.
7. Quoted in Schrödinger, *What is Life?*, pp. 206–8.
8. Jung, *Psychology and Religion*, p. 45.
9. Schrödinger, *What is Life?*, p. 218.
10. Jaspers, *The Great Philosophers*, p. 32.
11. Ibid., p. 36.
12. Schrödinger, *What is Life?*, p. 211.
13. Eliade, *Yoga, Freedom and Immortality*, p. 208.
14. Bottéro, *La Religion Babylonienne*, p. 51.
15. Coomaraswamy, *Buddha and the Gospel of Buddhism*, p. 201.
16. Quoted in Van der Leeuw, in *Man and Time*, ed. J. Campbell, p. 347.
17. Needham, *Science and Civilization in China*, vol. 2, pp. 290–1.
18. Quoted in Coulson, *Science and Christian Belief*, p. 27.
19. Windelband, *A History of Philosophy*, vol. 1, p. 146.
20. Coulson, *Science and Christian Belief*, p. 127.

21. Radhakrishnan, *Indian Philosophy*, vol.1 p. 441.
22. Ibid., p. 370.
23. Zimmer, *Philosophies of India*, p. 532.
24. Ibid., p. 284.
25. Quoted in Zaehner, *The Bhagavad-Gītā*, p. 49.
26. Quoted in Ibid., pp. 84–5.
27. Quoted in Zimmer, *Philosophies of India*, p. 386.
28. Quoted in Eliade, *Yoga, Freedom and Immortality*, p. 158.
29. Quoted in Zaehner, *Mysticism, Sacred and Profane*, p. 187.
30. Quoted in Ibid., p. 188.
31. *The Gospel of Ramakrishna*, ed. Swami Nikhilananda, p. 853.
32. Ibid., p. 915.
33. Eliade, *Yoga, Freedom and Immortality*, p. 160.
34. Zaehner, *The Bhagavad-Gītā*, p. 284.
35. John of the Cross, *The Ascent of Mount Carmel*, p. 3.
36. Quoted in Stace, *Religion and the Modern Mind*, p. 260.
37. Tresmontant, *La Métaphysique du Christianisme*, p. 249.
38. Ibid., p. 267.
39. Quoted in Schrödinger, *What is Life?*, p. 219.
40. Quoted in Stace, *Religion and the Modern Mind*, pp. 263–4.
41. Eliade, *Yoga, Freedom and Immortality*, p. 166.
42. Ibid., p. 179.

Chapter 4   SQUARING THE CIRCLE: BEYOND THE MIND

1. Rawlinson, *India*, p. 59.
2. Zimmer, *Philosophies of India*, p. 507.
3. Radhakrishnan, *Eastern Religions and Western Thought*, p. 21.
4. Quoted in Ogden and Richards, *The Meaning of Meaning*, p. 312.

5. Ibid., p. 317.
6. Unamuno, *The Tragic Sense of Life*, p. 34.
7. Ibid., p. 90.
8. Stace, *The Philosophy of Hegel*, p. 26.
9. Zimmer, *Philosophies of India*, p. 403.
10. Targ and Puthoff, *Mind-Reach*, p. 121.
11. *The World of Zen*, ed. N. W. Ross, p. 25.
12. *Albert Einstein, Philosopher–Scientist*, ed. P. A. Schilpp, p. 551.
13. Needham, *Science and Civilization in China*, vol. 2, p. 193.
14. Riencourt, *The Soul of China*, pp. 78–80.
15. Needham, *Science and Civilization in China*, vol. 2, p. 194.
16. Radhakrishnan, *Indian Philosophy*, vol. 1, p. 367.
17. Quoted in Ibid., p. 359.
18. Brown, *Wisdom of the Hindus*, p. 159.
19. Monier–Williams, *Brāhmanism and Hindūism*, p. 36.
20. Soulié de Morant, *L'Epopée des Jésuites Français en Chine*, pp. 214, 219.
21. *The Gospel of Ramakrishna*, ed. Swami Nikhilananda, p. 568.
22. John of the Cross, *The Dark Night of the Soul*, p. 28.

Chapter 5   MYSTICISM AS ART

1. Quoted in Jung, *Man and his Symbols*, pp. 253–63.
2. Tolstoy, *What is Art?*, p. 178.
3. Faure, *L'Art Antique*, p. XI.
4. Rodin, *L'Art*, p. 5.
5. Quoted in Zaehner, *Mysticism, Sacred and Profane*, p. 192.
6. *Encyclopedia of Religion and Ethics*, vol. 9, p. 709, ed. J. Hastings.

7. Smith, *Early Mysticism in the Near and Middle East*, p. 1.
8. Underhill, *Mysticism*, p. 58.
9. Zaehner, *Mysticism, Sacred and Profane*, pp. 156–60.
10. Underhill, *Mysticism*, p. 108.
11. Ibid., p. 64.
12. Ibid., p. 76.
13. Fülöp–Miller, *The Power and Secret of the Jesuits*, p. 13.
14. Bastide, *Les Problèmes de la Vie Mystique*, p. 53.
15. Ibid., pp. 58–9.
16. Ibid., p. 60.
17. Underhill, *Mysticism*, p. 84.
18. Ibid., p. 420.
19. Bastide, *Les Problèmes de la Vie Mystique*, p. 106.
20. Ibid., p. 106.
21. Ibid., p. 107.
22. Ibid., p. 108.
23. Ibid., p. 109.
24. Ibid., p. 116.
25. Ibid., p. 165.
26. Ibid., p. 167.
27. Underhill, *Mysticism*, p. 197.
28. Bastide, *Les Problèmes de la Vie Mystique*, p. 171.
29. Ibid., p. 173.
30. Ibid., p. 174.
31. Underhill, *Mysticism*, p. 194.
32. Ibid., p. 227.
33. Smith, *Early Mysticism in the Near and Middle East*, p. 53.

Chapter 6 MYSTICISM AS SCIENCE

1. Radhakrishnan, *Indian Philosophy*, vol. 2, p. 527.
2. Needham, *Science and Civilization in China*, vol. 2, p. 154.

3. Ibid., p. 37.
4. *The Legacy of India*, ed. G. T. Garratt, p. 62.
5. Ibid., p. 339.
6. Ibid., p. 339.
7. Radhakrishnan, *Indian Civilization*, vol. 1, p. 464.
8. Riencourt, *The Soul of India*, p. 39.
9. Ibid., pp. 41–2.
10. James, *The Varieties of Religious Experience*, pp. 298–9.
11. Riencourt, *The Soul of India*, p. 43.
12. Needham, *Science and Civilization in China*, vol. 2, p. 199.
13. Eliade, *Yoga, Immortality and Freedom*, p. 54.
14. Coomaraswamy, *Buddha and the Gospel of Buddhism*, p. 105.
15. Radhakrishnan, *Indian Philosophy*, vol. 1, p. 389.
16. Riencourt, *The Soul of India*, p. 45.
17. Monier–Williams, *Brāhmanism and Hindūism*, p. 35.
18. Eliade, *Yoga, Immortality and Freedom*, p. 57.
19. Quoted in Campbell, *The Mythic Image*, p. 379.
20. Eliade, *Yoga, Immortality and Freedom*, p. 270.
21. Ibid., p. 362.
22. Quoted in *Milarepa*, ed. W. Y. Evans–Wentz, p. 208.
23. Brown, *Life Against Death*, p. 208.
24. Blake, *Prophetic Writings*, vol. 1, p. 13.
25. Eliade, *Yoga, Immortality and Freedom*, p. 200.
26. Ibid., p. 228.
27. James, *The Varieties of Religious Experience*, p. 307.
28. Aurobindo, *The Synthesis of Yoga*, p. 3.
29. Quoted in Eliade, *Yoga, Freedom and Immortality*, p. 119.
30. Ibid., pp. 219–26.
31. Ibid., p. 216.
32. Needham, *Science and Civilization in China*, vol. 2, p. 454.
33. Eliade, *Yoga, Freedom and Immortality*, p. 232.

34. Needham, *Science and Civilization in China*, vol. 2, p. 428.
35. Rolland, *The Life of Ramakrishna*, pp. 162–3.
36. *The Gospel of Ramakrishna*, ed. Swami Nikhilananda, p. 29.
37. Herrigel, *Zen in the Art of Archery*, pp. 52–4.
38. Eliade, *Yoga, Freedom and Immortality*, pp. 72–3.
39. Ibid., p. 99.
40. *The Gospel of Ramakrishna*, ed. Swami Nikhilananda, p. 918.
41. Ibid., p. 733.
42. Rolland, *The Life of Vivekananda*, p. 190.
43. Herrigel, *Zen in the Art of Archery*, pp. 73–4.
44. Quoted in Eliade, *Yoga, Freedom and Immortality*, pp. 195–8.
45. Ibid., pp. 333–4.

Chapter 7 ORIENTALIZATION

1. Underhill, *Mysticism*, p. 189.
2. Ibid., p. 190.
3. Jeans, *Physics and Philosophy*, p. 143.
4. Frank, *Einstein*, p. 342.
5. Heisenberg, *Physics and Philosophy*, p. 76.
6. Ibid., p. 96.
7. Ibid., p. 128.
8. Ibid., p. 173.
9. Yukawa, *Creativity and Intuition*, p. 60.
10. Gardner, *The Ambidextrous Universe*, p. 249.
11. Ibid., p. 252.
12. Heisenberg, *Physics and Philosophy*, pp. 157–8.
13. Ibid., p. 160.
14. Ibid., pp. 154–5.
15. Oppenheimer, *Science and the Common Understanding*, pp. 42–3.

16. Carus, *The Gospel of Buddha*, p. XL.
17. Needham, *Science and Civilization in China*, vol. 2, p. 37.
18. Ibid., p. 194.
19. Ibid., p. 200.
20. Watts, *The Way of Zen*, p. 70.
21. Ibid., p. 71.
22. Zimmer, *Philosophies of India*, p. 513.
23. Watts, *The Way of Zen*, p. 72.
24. Schrödinger, *My View of the World*, p. 18.
25. Ibid., pp. 19–20.
26. Ibid., pp. 21–2.
27. Ibid., pp. 31 and 37.
28. Quoted in Needham, *Science and Civilization in China*, vol. 2, p. 46.
29. Schrödinger, *My View of the World*, p. 61.
30. Ibid., pp. 62–3.
31. Ibid., p. 64.
32. Ibid., p. 67.
33. Melsen, *From Atomos to Atoms*, p. 182.
34. Weizsäcker in introduction to Gopi Krishna, *The Biological Basis of Religion and Genius*, p. 44.
35. Einstein, *Out of my Later Years*, pp. 27–8.
36. Ibid., p. 25.
37. Ibid., p. 29.
38. Ibid., p. 26.
39. Hoyle, *The Nature of the Universe*, p. 124.
40. Russell, *The Autobiography of Bertrand Russell*, vol. 2, p. 160.

Chapter 8   CONVERGENCE

1. Riencourt, *The Soul of India*, p. 108.
2. Sullivan, *The Limitations of Science*, p. 126.
3. Sinnott, *Cell and Psyche*, p. 10.

4. Planck, *L'Image du Monde dans la Physique Moderne*, p. 129.
5. Ibid., p. 130.
6. Ibid., p. 129.
7. Targ and Puthoff, *Mind-Reach*, p. 119.
8. Ibid., p. 119. Also Ford, *The World of Elementary Particles*, pp. 203–4.
9. Targ and Puthoff, *Mind-Reach*, p. 170.
10. Planck, *L'Image du Monde dans la Physique Moderne*, pp. 131–2.
11. Ibid., pp. 132–3.
12. Ibid., p. 130.
13. Heisenberg, *Physics and Philosophy*, p. 135.
14. Peierls, *The Laws of Nature*, pp. 277–8.
15. Schrödinger, *What is Life?*, p. 17.
16. Sinnott, *Cell and Psyche*, p. 11.
17. Heisenberg, *Physics and Beyond*, p. 111.
18. Sinnott, *Cell and Psyche*, p. 29.
19. Thompson, *Passages about Earth*, p. 169.
20. Sinnott, *Cell and Psyche*, p. 41.
21. Ibid., p. 45.
22. Ibid., p. 49.
23. Ibid., p. 56.
24. Ibid., p. 78.
25. Ibid., p. 78.
26. Ibid., p. 79.
27. Eddington, *The Philosophy of Physical Science*, p. 181.
28. Gopi Krishna, *Kundalini*, pp. 12–13.
29. Ibid., pp. 48–50.
30. Ibid., p. 64.
31. Ibid., p. 66.
32. Ibid., p. 107.
33. Ibid., pp. 206–7.
34. Ibid., p. 207.
35. Ibid., p. 208.
36. Ibid., p. 210.

37. Rolland, *The Life of Vivekananda*, p. 219.
38. Ibid., p. 203.
39. Ibid., p. 219.
40. Gopi Krishna, *Kundalini*, p. 217.
41. Ibid., p. 241.
42. *The Integral Philosophy of Sri Aurobindo*, ed. H. Chaudhuri and F. Spiegelberg, p. 53.
43. Aurobindo, *The Ideal of Human Unity*, p. 310.
44. Ibid., p. 313.
45. Ibid., p. 314.
46. Ibid., p. 316.
47. Karan Singh, *Prophet of Indian Nationalism*, p. 85.
48. Gopi Krishna, *Higher Consciousness*, p. 48.
49. Weizsäcker in introduction to Gopi Krishna, *The Biological Basis of Religion and Genius*, p. 42.
50. Ibid., p. 43.

BIBLIOGRAPHY

Albert Einstein, Philosopher–Scientist, ed. P. A. Schilpp, New York, 1949.

AUROBINDO, S., *The Life Divine*, 2 vol., Pondicherry, 1970.

AUROBINDO, S., *The Synthesis of Yoga*, Pondicherry, 1971.

AUROBINDO, S., *The Ideal of Human Unity*, New York, 1950.

BARNETT, L., *The Universe and Dr. Einstein*, New York, 1948.

BASTIDE, R., *Les Problèmes de la Vie Mystique*, Paris, 1931.

BLAKE, W., *Prophetic Writings*, 2 vol., Oxford, 1926.

BOTTERO, J., *La Religion Babylonienne*, Paris, 1952.

BOURKE, V. J., *Aquinas' Search for Wisdom*, Milwaukee, 1965.

BROWN, N. O., *Life Against Death*, New York, 1959.

CAMPBELL, J., *The Masks of God: Primitive Mythology*, New York, 1959.

CAMPBELL, J., *The Mythic Image*, Princeton, 1974.

CAPEK, M., *The Philosophical Impact of Contemporary Physics*, Princeton, 1961.

CARUS, P., *The Gospel of Buddha*, London, 1915.

COOMARASWAMY, A., *Buddha and the Gospel of Buddhism*, London, 1928.

COULSON, C. A., *Science and Christian Belief*, London, 1964.

DANTE ALIGHIERI, *The Divine Comedy*, New York, 1932.

EDDINGTON, A. S., *The Nature of the Physical World*, Cambridge, 1931.

EDDINGTON, A. S., *The Philosophy of Physical Science*, New York, 1939.

EINSTEIN, A., *Out of my Later Years*, New York, 1950.

ELIADE, M., *Yoga, Freedom and Immortality*, London, 1958.

Encyclopedia of Religion and Ethics, ed. J. Hastings, New York, 1908–26, 13 vol.

FAURE, E., *Histoire de l'Art Antique*, Paris, 1921.

FORD, K. W., *The World of Elementary Particles*, New York, 1963.

FRANK, P., *Einstein*, London, 1949.

FRANKFORT, H. and H. A., *Before Philosophy*, Penguin, 1949.

FRAZER, J. G., *The Golden Bough*, New York, 1950.

FÜLÖP–MILLER, R., *The Power and Secret of the Jesuits*, New York, 1930.

GARDNER, M., *The Ambidextrous Universe*, New York, 1964.

The Gospel of Ramakrishna, ed. Swami Nikhilananda, New York, 1942.

GRANET, M., *La Pensée Chinoise*, Paris, 1950.

HEISENBERG, W., *Physics and Philosophy*, London, 1959.

HEISENBERG, W., *Physics and Beyond*, London, 1971.

HERRIGEL, E., *Zen in the Art of Archery*, London, 1956.

HOYLE, F., *The Nature of the Universe*, Penguin, 1963.

The Integral Philosophy of Sri Aurobindo, ed. H. Chaudhuri and F. Spiegelberg, London, 1960.

JAMES, W., *The Varieties of Religious Experience*, New York, 1958.

JASPERS, K., *The Great Philosophers*, New York, 1966.

JEANS, J., *Physics and Philosophy*, Cambridge, 1948.

JEANS, J., *The Mysterious Universe*, Cambridge, 1931.

JOHN OF THE CROSS, *The Ascent of Mount Carmel*, London, 1922.

JOHN OF THE CROSS, *The Dark Night of the Soul*, New York, 1957.

JUNG, C. G., *Psychology and Religion*, Yale, 1960.

JUNG, C. G., *Man and his Symbols*, New York, 1964.

KOESTLER, A., *The Roots of Coincidence*, London, 1972.

KRISHNA, G., *Kundalini*, London, 1971.

KRISHNA, G., *The Biological Basis of Religion and Genius*, New York, 1972.

KRISHNA, G., *Yoga, A Vision of its Future*, New Delhi, 1978.

KRISHNA, G., *Higher Consciousness*, New York, 1974.

The Legacy of India, ed. G. T. Garratt, Oxford, 1951.

LÉVI-STRAUSS, C., *La Pensée Sauvage*, Paris, 1962.

MELSEN, A. G., VAN, *From Atomos to Atom*, New York, 1960.

MONIER–WILLIAMS, M., *Brāhmanism and Hindūism*, London, 1887.

NEEDHAM, J., *Science and Civilization in China*, vol. 1 and vol. 2, Cambridge, 1954 and 1956.

OGDEN, C. K., and RICHARDS, I. A., *The Meaning of Meaning*, New York, 1923.

OPPENHEIMER, J. R., *Science and the Common Understanding*, Oxford, 1954.

PEIERLS, R. E., *The Laws of Nature*, London, 1957.

PLANCK, M., *L'Image du Monde dans la Physique Moderne*, Paris, 1963.

RADHAKRISHNAN, S., *Indian Philosophy*, 2 vol., London, 1956.

RADHAKRISHNAN, S., *Eastern Religions and Western Thought*, Oxford, 1940.

RAWLINSON, H. G., *India*, London, 1954.

REICHENBACH, H., *The Rise of Scientific Philosophy*, California U.P., 1951.

RIENCOURT, A. de, *The Soul of China*, London, 1959.

RIENCOURT, A. de, *The Soul of India*, London, 1961.

RODIN, A., *L'Art*, Paris, 1912.

ROLLAND, R., *The Life of Vivekananda*, Almora, 1953.

ROLLAND, R., *The Life of Ramakrishna*, Almora, 1954.

RUSSELL, B., *The autobiography of Bertrand Russell*, vol. 2, London, 1968.

SCHRÖDINGER, E., *What is Life?*, New York, 1956.

SCHRÖDINGER, E., *My View of the World*, Cambridge, 1964.

SINGH, K., *Prophet of Indian Nationalism*, Bombay, 1970.

SINNOTT, E. W., *Cell and Psyche*, New York, 1961.

SMITH, M., *Early Mysticism in the Near and Middle East*, New York, 1931.

SOULIÉ DE MORANT, G., *L'Epopée des Jésuites Français en Chine*, Paris, 1928.

STACE, W. T., *The Philosophy of Hegel*, New York, 1955.

STACE, W. T., *Religion and the Modern Mind*, New York, 1960.

SULLIVAN, J. W. N., *The Limitations of Science*, New York, 1961.

TARG, R., and PUTHOFF, H., *Mind-Reach*, London, 1977.

THOMPSON, W. I., *Passages about Earth*, New York, 1974.

The Tibetan Book of the Great Liberation, ed. W. Y. Evans–Wentz, Oxford, 1954.

Tibet's Great Yogi Milarepa, ed. W. Y. Evans–Wentz, Oxford, 1958.

TOLSTOY, L., *What is Art?*, Oxford, 1950.

TRESMONTANT, C., *La Métaphysique du Christianisme*, Paris, 1961.

TRESMONTANT, C., *Comment se Pose Aujourd'hui le Problème de l'Existence de Dieu*, Paris, 1966.

UNAMUNO, M., *Tragic Sense of Life*, New York, 1954.

UNDERHILL, E., *Mysticism*, New York, 1956.

VAN DER LEEUW, G., in *Man and Time*, ed. J. Campbell, London, 1958.

WATTS, A. W., *The Way of Zen*, London, 1957.

WIGNER, E. P., *Symmetries and Reflections*, Cambridge, Mass., 1970.

WINDELBAND, W., *A History of Philosophy*, 2 vol., New York, 1958.

The World of Zen, ed. N. W. Ross, New York, 1960.

YUKAWA, H., *Creativity and Intuition*, Tokyo, 1973.

ZAEHNER, R. C., *Mysticism, Sacred and Profane*, Oxford, 1957.

ZAEHNER, R. C., *The Bhagavad-Gitā*, Oxford, 1973.

ZIMMER, H., *Philosophies of India*, ed. J. Campbell, London, 1951.

INDEX